ASIAN REFLECTIONS ON THE AMERICAN LANDSCAPE:

IDENTIFYING AND INTERPRETING ASIAN HERITAGE

Brian D. Joyner

Office of Diversity and Special Projects

National Center for Cultural Resources

National Park Service

U.S. Department of the Interior

2005

Table of Contents

Executive Summary

Asian Reflections on the American Landscape: Identifying and Interpreting Asian Heritage **highlights the cultural imprint of Asian groups on the built environment of the United States. It is part of an effort by the National Park Service and its partners to increase the awareness of the historic places associated with the nation's cultural and ethnic groups that have been identified, documented, recognized, and interpreted and to lay the groundwork for the identification of additional historic places. Many of the examples in this publication are drawn from National Park Service cultural resources programs that are carried out in partnership with other government agencies and private organizations.**

Documented Asian contact with the North American continent dates back to at least to the middle of the 16th century. Asian ethnic groups participated in the early settlement of the United States, contributed to the economic development of the American West, and played a role in the desegregation of public schools in the United States in the 20th century. Aspects of Asian cultures influence our language, our palette, and our landscape. Studies of Asian American culture began in earnest during the middle of the 20th century. Scholars are increasingly documenting the role of Asians in American cultural life and the impact of discriminatory legislation on Asian communities in the United States.

This examination of Asian cultures in the United States occurs as the number of people of Asian descent is rapidly increasing. Census data indicates the Asian population has grown 48 percent since the 1990 census, as compared to 13 percent for the general population. However, Asian groups have a heterogeneity that makes the all-inclusive administrative construct of "Asian American" deceiving. Older established communities such as Chinese and Japanese Americans are making way for newer communities of Vietnamese and Cambodian Americans. The

Pacific Islander population is considered part of this group. This constantly evolving demographic is making its influence felt in all aspects of American life.

The publication is intended to support the efforts of historic preservation and cultural resource stewardship professionals and organizations within their communities. It is intended for the general reader, one without specific knowledge of Asian or Asian American cultural heritage. This document includes:

- An introductory essay that summarizes Asian cultural heritage in the United States
- An annotated list of historic properties related to Asian cultural heritage that are listed in the National Register of Historic Places listings, designated as National Historic Landmarks, and documented by the Historic American Buildings Survey/Historic American Engineering Record, all programs of the National Park Service
- Examples of historic places that interpret aspects of Asian heritage for the public benefit
- A list of historic properties documented and/or recognized by National Park Service cultural resources programs, arranged by program and state
- A bibliography containing well-known and accessible publications on the topic

Asian Reflection on the American Landscape: Identifying and Interpreting Asian Heritage is the second publication by the National Park Service using this methodology to highlight the imprint of diverse groups on the built environment of the United States. The first volume, *African Reflection on the American Landscape: Identifying and Interpreting Africanisms*, was published in 2003.

Acknowledgments

This publication is the second volume in a series of publications that highlights the impact of the nation's cultural and ethnic groups on the American built environment. The first volume in this series was African Reflections on the American Landscape: Identifying and Interpreting Africanisms, *which was published in 2003. The African Reflections publication provided a successful model for examining diverse cultural groups and their impact upon the built environment. It was produced to encourage preservation professionals to seek additional examples in their own communities. This volume similarly provides examples of Asian heritage and lays the groundwork for additional exploration of this topic.*

Identifying and Interpreting Asian Heritage was produced under the direction of Antoinette J. Lee, special projects manager, National Center for Cultural Resources. Michèle Gates Moresi, historian, National Center for Cultural Resources, provided critical input on bibliographic sources and methodology, as well as editorial support throughout the numerous drafts. This publication benefited greatly from research undertaken by interns Daphne Dador and Janet Paz. We appreciate the cooperation of Eloisa Borah, Lucy Cohen, Kevin Foster, Laura Feller, Marilyn Harper, John Muir, Franklin Odo, Martin Perschler, Mark Pfeifer, Carol Shull, Erika Martin Seibert, John Sprinkle, Dan Vivian, Priscilla Wegars, and Frank Wu—all of whom reviewed and offered crucial editorial comment on the manuscript. In addition, Lawrence Kingsbury and Dwight Pitcaithley suggested bibliographic resources that contributed to the final document.

Asia in America:
AN INTRODUCTION

America has always been a place of ethnic diversity. However, since the 1950s and especially after changes in immigration laws in 1965, the range of people joining the cultural mosaic has grown at an astounding rate. The United States boasts significant numbers of people from well over 100 countries. The census rolls and demographic makeup of school districts reflect this increase in diverse people, with the percentage of the diverse population climbing toward 50 percent of the total population and literally dozens of languages being spoken at some schools in urban areas.

One region of the world that contributes heavily to the nation's increasing diversity is Asia. As long as there has been a "new world," Asia and its people have been involved in its development. Among the earliest travelers to the Americas were people of Asian descent. While Europe and Africa provided the larger percentage of the nation's early immigrants, Asia and the Pacific Islands have contributed to the North American experience since the late 1500s. The Asian and North American continents are linked through their people and their roles in the Age of Exploration. When European explorers searching for quicker routes to India and other Asian markets found themselves in North America, they encountered descendants of earlier migrations from the Asian continent.[1] As the Western world was seeking new ways to reach Asia, Asia was already exploring the West.[2]

The desire for wealth, trade, and land starting in the 15th century led several European nations to the seas in search of new opportunities. Regions of Asia and Africa were the focus of early imperial endeavors. India was an area of commercial interest for centuries, providing much of the impetus for transoceanic voyages. The technological innovations of the Chinese (medicinal herbs and building material, such as "rammed earth") and the various textile and mineral resources of the Asian continent and the surrounding island nations were chronicled in the tales of Marco Polo and by travelers along the trade routes that stretched from Venice to Xian. Eventually, attempts to find shorter routes to Asian trading depots and new markets brought ships to the Western Hemisphere and the New World. Spain saw the strategic importance of the Pacific Islands upon landing in the Philippines in 1521 and establishing a permanent settlement in 1565.[3] Beginning in the 16th century, European explorers and settlers embarked on expeditions to the nascent shores of the North American continent to develop colonies for economic exploitation.

Sailors from the Philippines and China are reported to have sailed with Spanish galleons along the routes between Manila and Spanish ports in Louisiana, California, Mexico, and Panama. Filipinos were among the landing party at Morro Bay, California, with Pedro de Unamumo in 1587.[4] Chinese sailors were employed in the shipping trades in New England and the Pacific Northwest in the 1800s. Asian immigrants participated in the development of the western United States. Chinese workers helped to create the transcontinental railroad and were instrumental in linking the western spur of the Central Pacific railroad across extremely treacherous terrain. Asian Indians, Japanese, and Chinese immigrants labored in lumber camps in the West during the mid-to-late 19th century. Koreans, Japanese, Filipinos, and Chinese worked in the agricultural industries in Hawaii and California.

■ The story of Chinese labor in the completion of the transcontinental railroad is a critical one in our understanding of westward expansion. The North Pacific Coast Railroad employed Chinese laborers, pictured in 1898, as section hands in Corte Madera.

Courtesy of the California Historical Society

■ Filipino and Chinese laborers worked side-by-side with Mexican and European American migrant laborers to build the agricultural wealth of the Central Valley area of California. These laborers harvested bell peppers, lettuce, celery, artichoke, and asparagus crops, ca. 1950s.

Courtesy of the Alvarado Project

The history of Asians in America is not limited to labor history. Chinese students arrived on American shores as early as 1847. Filipino students or *pensionados*, and Japanese students attended American schools, colleges, and universities in the late 19th-to-early 20th centuries. Filipino soldiers participated in the Battle of New Orleans. During the Civil War, Chinese soldiers fought for the Union Army. Japanese, Korean, Chinese, and Filipino soldiers and seamen served with distinction in the American Armed Forces in both World Wars. The 442nd Regimental Combat Team, a segregated Japanese American unit, was the most highly decorated unit of its size in World War II. Cambodians, Laotians, and Vietnamese arrived in Massachusetts, Texas, and Minnesota during and following the Vietnam War. In the latter part of the 20th century, a new generation of Asian Indian immigrants arrived with technological and managerial expertise in medicine and in the information services field. Asian communities are found in diverse locales in the United States, from New York to Mississippi and Washington State.

■ The Filipino Varsity Four was a musical group comprised of Filipino college students, known as *pensionados*, sponsored by the Federal Government to study in the United States.

Courtesy of Records of the Redpath Chautauqua Collection, Special Collections Department, University of Iowa

The term, "Asian American" emerged in the 1960s, fueled by the same civil rights issues driving other minority groups to seek equal representation within American society. Asian American students no longer wanted to be called Asiatic or Oriental, but wanted a phrase that represented their ethnic heritage and their American roots. People of Asian descent engaged the political and educational establishment in the same manner as young African Americans and Hispanic Americans. In 1968, San Francisco State College, now San Francisco State University, and the University of California at Berkeley were the first institutions of higher education to offer Asian American Studies programs. This period also coincides with the lifting of numerical quotas for ethnic immigrants with the 1965 amendment to the Immigration and Nationality Act of 1952.

American culture is filled with Asian cultural legacies. To cite a few, Japanese horticultural techniques influence our diets and physical landscape. Chinese life-saving practices, developed in the 18th century, have become universalized and are common practice for shipping and sailing. Practices regarding our physical and spiritual well-being are infused with pan-Asian cultural aspects, from Buddhism to martial arts and yoga. Japanese architectural aesthetics influenced Frank Lloyd Wright's Prairie style. A Filipino immigrant, Pedro Flores, brought a standard bearer of popular culture, the yo-yo and its subsequent popularity, to the United States. Words of Asian origin color our language. The term boondocks, for instance, is derived from the Tagalog term "bundok" meaning mountain, but in American usage it describes a hinterland or remote backcountry. It entered the English language during the Philippine-American War.

This document provides an overview of the influence of Asian heritage on the cultural landscape of the United States. Using National Park Service resources, it offers a summary of scholarship on Asian heritage in America, provides examples of Asian heritage that have been identified in National Park Service programs, presents examples of interpretation of Asian cultures at historic sites, includes a select listing of bibliographic references, and lists Asian sites and properties that the National Park Service cultural resources programs have recognized and interpreted. This study by no means represents an exhaustive exploration of the topic. It serves as an introduction to the topic of Asian ethnicity in the United States and how it manifests itself in the nation's cultural resources.

Who are "Asians?"

"Asians" come from the areas of southern, central, and eastern Asia, and from islands that lie within the Pacific Rim. This region is bordered by Russia to the north, and by Afghanistan, Tajikistan, Kyrgyzstan, and Kazakhstan to the west. To the southwest, it is bordered by the Indian Ocean and to the east, the Pacific Ocean. People from China, Japan, Korea, the Philippines, India, Cambodia, Vietnam, Laos, Thailand, Taiwan, Malaysia, Indonesia, Singapore, and Brunei fall under the category of "Asian."[5] Groups from the Pacific Islands—such as Hawaii, the Marshall Islands, Guam, American Samoa, and the Mariana Islands—represent a related group. Some institutions link Asian Americans and Pacific Islanders. Others, such as the U.S. Census Bureau, treat them as separate entities.

The Chee Kong Tong House, pictured in 1966, was a meeting place for Chinese from the same district living in Maui.

Photograph by Jack E. Boucher, courtesy of the Historic American Buildings Survey

Through the Asian diaspora, their communities can be found throughout the world. Asian communities extend across the Pacific Ocean; through the Pacific Islands and Australia; into Canada, Mexico, and the United States; through Central America and the Caribbean Islands, in places such as Trinidad and Tobago; and into South America, in Peru and Brazil. Korean communities exist in Japan, Chinese communities exist in Taiwan, and Asian Indian communities are located in South Africa and Fiji. Vietnamese communities exist in Australia; roughly one million Japanese immigrated to Brazil during the 1920s; Chinese communities have been long established in Jamaica, Cuba, and Peru.

The Chinese, Japanese, Filipinos, Koreans, and Asian Indians were among the earliest to immigrate in significant numbers and constitute the largest Asian groups that settled in the United States. These five Asian immigrant groups shaped the cultural landscape in California, Washington, Hawaii, and in major metropolitan areas like New York, Los Angeles, and Chicago. In particular, Hawaii is a key site of diaspora for Asian groups. As late as 1970, 50 percent of the Asian American population was in Hawaii. According to census data, 25 percent of the counties in the nation with Asian Americans as the majority are in Hawaii and 68 percent of the population of Honolulu is of Asian descent.[6]

A detail of the Chee Kong Tong House's porch in 1966 displays the Chinese influence on its construction.

Photograph by Jack E. Boucher, courtesy of the Historic American Buildings Survey

■ Located in Falls Church, VA, the Eden Center, shown in 2003, with its restaurants and specialty shops serves as a hub of activity for the local Vietnamese community.

Courtesy of Marcia Axtmann Smith

Since 1975 and the fall of Saigon, Vietnamese, Cambodians, and Laotians have arrived in increasing numbers. The Vietnamese, in particular, have raised the number of Asian-descended people and altered the landscape of where Asian Americans settle. Whereas California is still the primary place of settlement for all Asian groups in America; Texas, not Hawaii, is the second choice for Vietnamese and Laotians. Cambodians carved out an identity in Massachusetts, and the Hmong community gathered in Minnesota.[7] Smaller Asian immigrant groups, such as Thais and Indonesians, are becoming better recognized. These developments changed the dynamic in Asian American communities, where the older communities formerly dominated much of the debate about people of Asian descent in America.

The AAPI Population in the United States

As of the 2000 Census, the Asian American/Pacific Islander population (AAPI) in the United States numbered 12 million people, or 4.3% of the total population. The Asian population has grown at a faster rate than the total population—up 48% since the last census as compared with 13% for the general population.[8] Recent immigration patterns have altered the picture of Asian peoples in the United States. The largest groups are Chinese at 2.3 million, Filipinos at 2.1 million, Asian Indians at 1.9 million, Koreans at 1.3 million, and Vietnamese at 1.2 million. The Japanese, formerly one of the five most populous ethnicities, are now sixth at 1.1 million.[9] Native Hawaiians/Pacific Islanders number 874,000 people. The six largest Asian ethnic groups make up 83% of the total Asian-American/Pacific Islander population.[10]

The place of Pacific Islanders in the Asian American mosaic has been debated. As past and present American territories, the Pacific Islands fall into an ambiguous category that is neither foreign nor American. The state of Hawaii represents the dichotomy of Pacific Islanders. Its status as a state allows it a voice beyond that of the territories. Hawaii presents very much a different view of "America," one where the syncretic pan-Asian culture is a visible part of the cultural landscape and contributes to its sense of place.

Asian Presence in America

According to William S. Bernard, professor emeritus of sociology at Brooklyn College, immigration to the Americas is divided into five periods: the Colonial Period (1607-1775), with Asian settlements reported as early as 1765 [11]; the Open Door Period (1776-1881),

1 shows front curtain as
it was at time of apprehension.
2. shows box with kitchen
utensils where revolver
was found.
~~~~~~~~~~~ed box where
~~~~~~~~~nd.

■ Prohibitions on immigration
forced Chinese and other Asians
to resort to smuggling themselves
across the Mexican border into
the U.S. This ca. 1921 photograph
of a smuggling buggy was used
as evidence in a federal case
against individuals illegally
assisting Chinese migrants.

Courtesy of the National Archives
Records Administration

when Asians arrived in the new nation, eager to stake a claim to the country's wealth and prosperity; the Regulation Period (1882-1916), where concerns over Asian assimilation to American culture led to legislated discrimination against Asians; the Restriction Period (1917-1964), which saw housing covenants and other restrictions against Asian groups become prevalent; and the Liberalization Period (1965-present), with the removal of quotas and legal impediments to Asian immigration and the beginning of the process of greater assimilation of Asians into American culture.[12]

As with many immigrant groups, the initial wave of Asian immigrants arrived in the United States to fulfill the need for labor. Sugar masters were brought to Hawaii in the 1830s and Chinese sailors and peddlers are reported in New York around the same time.[13] Later, Chinese were brought to Hawaii to work on the sugar and pineapple plantations. Thus began a pattern of United States importation of Asians to fulfill labor needs throughout the 19th and early 20th centuries. Workers were recruited, primarily from districts in the Guangdong province of southern China, to Hawaii and later California. Districts like Sam Yup and Sze Yap have sizable populations in North America and formed associations to support fellow migrants.

The discovery of gold in California attracted the majority of early Chinese immigrants to the United States. Chinese miners spread throughout California, Nevada, Oregon, Montana, and Idaho, and planned to earn money and return to their home province.[14] Most never became rich or returned home. Laws and taxes making mining for Chinese cost-prohibitive, combined with physical coercion, ensured that most would never achieve the promise of *gum saan* or "Gold Mountain."[15] As mining became less lucrative, Chinese immigrants explored other opportunities. Thousands worked on the Central Pacific portion of the transcontinental railroad, along with thousands more recruited from China. Others became merchants, catering to the tastes of the growing Chinese communities.

Migrant farm labor, lumber mills, and logging camps offered other opportunities. Chinese sailors contributed to the shipping trade in New England and Chinese junks harvested shrimp out of San Francisco Bay. However, western states viewed the immigrants as competitors for jobs and for land, and began legislating Chinese to the margins of society. More and more laws designed to curtail the

■ Chinese benevolent societies, made up of people from the same province or speaking the same dialect, attended to matters when family was not present, such as the burial service of High Lee, 1891, in Deadwood, SD.

Courtesy of John C. H. Grabill Collection, Prints and Photographs Division, Library of Congress

influx of Chinese eventually led to the Chinese Exclusion Act of 1882.[16] But the need for labor to build the country only increased and other groups were sought.

Japanese immigrants first arrived in America between 1868 and 1869 when a group of businessmen spirited out 100 Japanese to perform agricultural labor in Hawaii, Guam, and California.[17] Subsequent waves of Japanese migrated from a small number of prefectures in the southwest of Japan. Hiroshima, Yamaguchi, Okayama, Wakayama prefectures on Honshu Island, and Fukuoka, Kumamoto, Nagasaki, Saga, and Kagoshima prefectures on Kyushu Island provided the overwhelming majority of Japanese migrants to the Asian diaspora.[18] Arriving as contract workers in the wake of the Chinese Exclusion Act of 1882, the Japanese worked the sugar industry until the Organic Act of 1900 made the immigration of foreign nationals as contract labor illegal. Railroads, lumber mills, and farms in California and Washington formed the next stage of settlement for Japanese immigrants. However, the Gentlemen's Agreement of 1907 further curtailed their immigration.

Many Japanese immigrants carved out a niche in agriculture and horticulture. Early Japanese immigrants to California arrived with mulberry trees, silkworm cocoons, tea plants, bamboo roots, and other products, and became heavily involved with the burgeoning agricultural labor movement during the 1920s and 1930s.

World War II changed the dynamic of relationships between Japanese Americans and the rest of the nation. Executive Order 9066 paved the way for the removal of all persons of Japanese descent from western coastal areas to internment camps in the interior of the country. This policy effectively eliminated many of the Japantowns and other Japanese enclaves that sustained Japanese and Japanese American culture. These areas would never fully recover. Later, postwar urban renewal and highway act projects would finish what internment had begun by putting roads and highways through Japanese American neighborhoods (and other minority neighborhoods), further disintegrating the cultural essence of those places.[19] Many Japanese chose either to relocate to the Midwest or move to the East Coast.

Korean immigration to the United States began in 1903, with the arrival of a group of Korean men to Honolulu, Hawaii, to perform agricultural work on the plantations.[20] Similar to the Chinese and

Japanese before them, early Korean communities were primarily bachelor enclaves, whose members were intent on earning enough money to return home as wealthy men. Unlike their predecessors, Koreans came from no particular region in Korea. Those present in the country continued agricultural work on sugar plantations in Hawaii and rice cultivation in California. Others found work as laborers in lumber yards in Washington state and in canneries in Alaska. Several became merchants and opened stores. Christian Korean congregations were the earliest of institutions to be formed, along with language schools.[21]

The attempts at exploitation of Korean immigrants in the American labor markets were curtailed due to Japanese opposition.[22] Combined with the restrictive quota on the immigrants of Asian origin due to the Immigration Act of 1924, it would be 40 years before Korean immigration would begin in earnest. Korean immigration increased after World War II, when some 6,000 women entered the country as brides of United States military men.[23] The 1965 amendment to the Immigration and Nationality Act encouraged further growth. Enclaves developed throughout the nation, primarily in New York, Los Angeles, and Seattle.

Although small groups of Asian Indians first arrived on the shores of the United States in the 1790s, Asian Indian immigration to North America began in the 1890s.[24] Asian Indians emigrated initially to British Columbia. This was curtailed by a series of anti-Asian legislation in Canada beginning in 1900. They began entering the United States through Bellingham, Washington. Asian Indians briefly filled the void left by the Japanese in 1907 with the signing of the Gentleman's Agreement until passage of the Barred Zone Act of 1917. Although some arrived illegally through Mexico, their numbers did not increase substantially until the 1970s.

Early Asian Indian migrants were primarily from the Punjab region and of Sikh faith, but many were Muslim and Hindu as well. As with other Asian groups, the first waves of Asian Indians fulfilled unskilled labor needs, settling in California, Washington, and Oregon. However, since 1965, Asian Indian immigration increased and included a sizable percentage of highly skilled professionals, particularly in the information technology and medical fields.[25] Asian Indian communities are found in Maryland, Louisiana, New Jersey, and Massachusetts.

■ Over 1 million people of Asian descent entered the United States through the Angel Island Immigration Center in San Francisco Bay. Asian Indians, such as these pictured ca. 1916, were among them.

Courtesy of California State Department of Parks and Recreation

Already a presence the United States, the immigration of Filipinos increased sharply to fulfill the need for workers in Hawaii starting in 1906. The unique status of the Philippines as an American territory allowed Filipinos to travel on American passports, making them attractive to the Hawaiian agricultural industry after the passing of the Organic Act of 1900. Filipino agricultural workers were heavily involved with the growing labor union movement, and cooperated with Japanese and Hispanic workers on strikes in Hawaii and California. In 1930, the Agricultural Workers League was formed in California to provide Pinoy—the name for Filipinos in the United States—workers with the same bargaining power as European American workers.[26] During the 1960s, Filipino workers and unions supported César Chávez, the celebrated labor organizer, and participated in the United Farm Workers of America demonstrations in Delano, California.

A former colony of Spain and United States, the Philippines has a culture more hybridized than other Asian cultures. Although Philippine independence from United States control occurred on July 4, 1946, American cultural influence still exists. Because of their hybrid culture, Filipinos find themselves considered neither American nor Asian.[27] Today, Filipinos are one of the fastest growing Asian groups in America.

Pacific Islanders are indigenous peoples from the island chains that spread from Australia to Hawaii. The Pacific Islands (as related to the United States) include the Northern Mariana Islands, Guam, American Samoa, Hawaii, the Marshall Islands, and the Federated States of Micronesia. Each group of islands existed as independent states or loose federations of culturally connected peoples prior to the arrival of Europeans, starting with Ferdinand Magellan in 1521.[28] These encounters, which eventually led Asians to the North American continent, spread multiple Asian peoples throughout the Pacific Islands. Hawaii, in particular, has been a site of diaspora for Chinese, Japanese, Koreans, Filipinos, and other Pacific Islanders.

While immigration to and among the Pacific Islands dates back millennia, emigration to the mainland is of a shorter duration.[29] Three hundred Hawaiian contract workers were employed by the Hudson's Bay Company at Fort Vancouver in Washington State during the mid-19th century. A village of diverse peoples within the trading post walls became known as Kanaka Village, a Hawaiian term for "person".[30] Beyond this, however, there is little research on Pacific Islander migration, although American Samoan and Chamorro people have immigrated to the mainland in traceable numbers since the mid-20th century.[31] Aspects of Hawaiian culture are recognizable within American cultural heritage, but it too, suffers from the distance between the islands and the mainland. How to define the place of Pacific Islanders within Asian American culture is a subject of ongoing discussion among scholars and preservation professionals.

■ The Vedanta Society provided a place of worship for followers of Vedantism, a branch of Hinduism, in San Francisco, CA. It is a rare example of Hindu architectural style in the United States.

[No photographer or date in file] Courtesy of the Historic American Buildings Survey

Asian Influence on the Cultural Landscape

Throughout the United States, Asian groups have made an impact on the cultural landscape. Many buildings, landscapes, archeological resources, and much material culture found in the United States today reflect cultural connections to Asia. The multiple Asian groups in the Hawaiian Islands developed agricultural practices that influenced the growth of sugar, pineapple, and rice. Ethnic enclaves in many areas bore marks of the groups through businesses and organizations, aesthetic choices, signage, and cultural arts.

Houses of worship are prime examples of Asian-influenced buildings. The institutions associated with the faiths offer insights into cultural practices that connect back to the respective places of origin. Buddhism, for example, reportedly arrived with Japanese immigrants in the 1870s. Buddhist temples, such as the Kawailoa Temple in Hawaii, served not only their community's spiritual needs, but they functioned equally well as schools and places of social gathering. Shinto shrines, with their unique building techniques, and Hindu gudwaras served as boarding houses as well as houses of worship for Asian Indian travelers. Christian churches offered spiritual support for Asian communities. The Chinese Community Church in Washington, DC, served as a spiritual guide

■ The Friendship Archway is a gift to the Chinese American community in Washington, DC, from the People's Republic of China. The archway, shown in 2003, was assembled using an architectural technique called dou gong, which uses carved wood fitting together like a jigsaw puzzle without nails or screws.

Courtesy of Marcia Axtmann Smith

■ The Southeast Asian Water Festival draws thousands of spectators each year to the Merrimack River. The flyer from the 2002 festival is an example of how Cambodian community has interwoven itself into the fabric of the city of Lowell, MA.

Courtesy of Lowell National Historic Park

for nearly 40 years, and still serves the Chinatown community as a place of gathering. Other churches and places of worship around the country may possess cultural heritage associations. For example, Korean community churches, particularly in places such as Hawaii, serve a spiritual and secular role in Korean communities, providing a social framework as well as being a receptacle for cultural traditions.[32]

For much of the 20th century, ethnic enclaves offered tangible evidence of the legal and economic impediments to broader housing choices for Asians. Brightly colored buildings, adorned with Chinese calligraphic signage, animalized columns, and statues are immediately recognizable as features of a Chinatown. The spirit of Chinese heritage is evident, whether the buildings are Queen Anne row houses or warehouses. Little Tokyos, Koreatowns, Chinatowns, and Little Manilas represent a visual affirmation of place for the Asian immigrant communities. Within many of the enclaves are language schools and community centers.

Lowell National Historical Park in Massachusetts is known for its connection to the rise of the industrial age in the United States. However, an emerging Cambodian community has become one of the park's primary users. The park management has encouraged a partnership between the community and the park, giving the park significance beyond its original association with the 19th-century Industrial Revolution. Lowell provides an example of a new community attaching its own cultural and historic significance to an established historic site.

The Presidio of San Francisco has a different and more difficult historic attachment for Japanese Americans. When the United States entered World War II, its government ordered the removal of people of Japanese ancestry from western coastal regions. At the same time, the Army recruited second-generation Japanese Americans, or *nisei*, to teach Japanese to military personnel and provide support in deciphering documents and interrogating captives. The resulting Military Intelligence Service Language School was housed at the Presidio in Building 640. Through its association with the Presidio's military history, this bittersweet chapter of America's recent past is highlighted and examined.

■ The map shows the various internment camps and assembly centers throughout the country associated with the internment of people of Japanese descent during World War II. These camps housed Japanese Americans who were forcibly removed from the West Coast of the United States.

Courtesy of the National Park Service

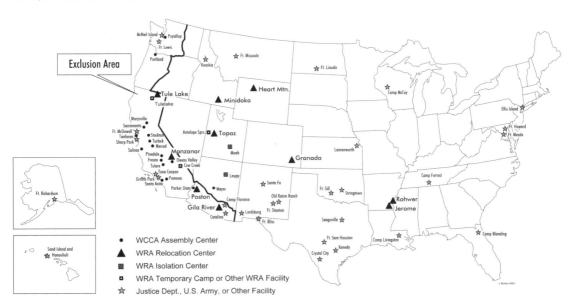

The "Invisibility" of Asian Cultural Heritage in America

The remarkable length of duration of Asian ethnicities in the United States has not translated into visibility in American culture comparable to European groups. Members of the community and publications have underscored this lack of presence.[33] This "invisibility" is not limited to Asian ethnicities, but is particularly relevant to any discussion of the impact of Asian cultural heritage on the built environment.

While Asian influences permeate American culture, they have often been overlooked by the nation at large. The nation's historically acknowledged practices of exclusion, segregation, and discrimination kept the population small and segregated relative to the rest of the population. Immigration quotas and legal impediments to citizenship prevented a critical mass of Asian people from gaining a greater foothold. Successive Asian groups were prevented from owning property due to local and state legislation. Law against intermarriage and the prohibition of most Asian female immigration during the early part of the 20th century ensured bachelor communities with a low rate of population increase.[34] These barriers curtailed the intercultural melding of heritage that occurred with European communities.

Looking at places of cultural memory among Asian Americans requires a careful interpretation of space, defined as much by what is gone as by what exists, and by who claims it rather than by who controls it.

The experiences of people within an environment are what define space for individuals or groups. Ethnic enclaves, while obscuring the groups from the larger public sphere, reinforce an intracultural experience distinct to those locations and individuals.[35] Locations of former ethnic enclaves are equally important for the residents. Looking at places of cultural memory among Asian Americans requires a careful interpretation of space, defined as much by what is gone as by what exists, and by who claims it rather than by who controls it. Asian American sites of cultural memory frequently bear no markers or may represent contested space within rural and urban landscapes.[36] As more of these places disappear and their residents pass away, those memories fade from the public consciousness and this part of American culture remains invisible.

Other factors, such as cultural differences, contribute to the lack of a physical presence of Asian heritage in the American built environment. For example, some Asian cultures do not place the same importance on older structures as Western preservationists. In Japan, Shinto shrines are ritualistically and periodically rebuilt to receive blessings from the gods. No one would question the significance of the religious site in Japan, but it is difficult to make a case for integrity in considering their eligibility for local, state, or federal historic registers in the United States. These cultural differences have created difficulties in documenting and preserving some places of Asian heritage because they do not meet official designation criteria.[37] National Register-eligible archeological sites related to Asian heritage do exist such as the Chinese sites in the Warren Mining District near McCall, Idaho, or the Takahashi Farm outside of Sacramento, California. These sites contain material and structural remnants of Asian heritage on the built environment of the nation.[38]

Recent studies of ethnic minorities in the United States suggest that Asian groups possess a strong sense of place.[39] Diverse people such as Asian Americans are often deemed to be "foreign" no matter how many generations lived in America.[40] This belief affects how preservation professionals view and interpret historic places that may have multiple histories to present. An examination of the historic record, notably South Asians in port cities throughout the East Coast during the 18th century, the roles of Chinese and Japanese settlers in the development of the American West, and the presence of Filipinos in Louisiana challenges these notions.[41]

Scholarship on Asians in America

Much of the scholarly writing on Asian Americans addresses the individual groups. Early studies included detailed histories on the Chinese and Japanese in chronicling the development of their communities. Immigration and assimilation studies dominated the early discussions, frequently led by scholars outside of the Asian American community. Moreover, there were few, if any, specialists in the field of Asian American cultural studies. The first publication on an Asian American ethnic group written by a native-born member of the community was *The Chinese in the United States of America*, by sociologist Rose Hum Lee in 1960.[42] She was concerned with the loss of Chinese culture among American-born Chinese.

Examinations of the significance of place focus on enclaves: Chinatowns, Little Saigons, and Japantowns or *nihonmachi*. Architect and historian Christopher Yip examined Chinatowns in his studies of the town of Locke, a farming community in the Sacramento Valley,[43] and viewed the enclaves as expressions of traditional culture on the landscape. Gail Dubrow documented Japanese immigrants throughout Washington State. Her most recent work, *Sento at Sixth and Main* (with Donna Graves), highlights important sites of West Coast Japanese American heritage.[44]

Another important thread in contemporary scholarship on Asian Americans is the role that legal and de facto discrimination played. Laws dating from 1790 served to legislate Asian minorities out of the mainstream by limiting their access to American institutions and excluding them from citizenship. Asian communities opposed these laws, leaving a written record of their struggle for equality. Documentary evidence that includes court records, newspapers, and local, state, and federal legislation, provides rich resources for scholars. Franklin Odo's *The Columbia Documentary History of the Asian American Experience* contains transcripts of discriminatory legislation and the judicial battles waged against it.[45]

Viewing Asian American culture through the lens of social justice and systematic disenfranchisement became a focus of academic study starting in the early 20th century. Mary Roberts Coolidge's *Chinese Immigration*, published in 1909, addressed the issues underlying labor and discrimination against Chinese, culminating with her "California thesis," which points to volatile contentions over wealth and power in California as the root of the government's discriminatory legislation.[46] Hers is one of the earliest examinations of the matter and is considered to be a seminal text on labor and immigration history.

Historian Sucheng Chan wrote about Chinese communities in California as well as the larger Asian American population. Her *Asian Americans: An Interpretative History* is a cornerstone in Asian American scholarship, and *This Bittersweet Soil: The Chinese in California Agriculture, 1860-1910*, published in 1991, looks at the impact of Chinese immigrants on California's rapidly developing agribusiness sector at the turn of the 20th century.[47] Public historian Him Mark Lai extensively researched the history of the Chinese in America. Based on his research of Chinese language newspapers and communities around the country, *A History Reclaimed: An Annotated Bibliography of Chinese Language Materials on the Chinese of America* was published in 1986.[48]

Historian Gary Okihiro looked at various Asian American histories, most recently in *The Columbia Guide to Asian American History* published in 2001.[49] The text summarizes the range of historical topics and areas of scholarship affecting the on-going interpretation of the history Asians in America. A professor of Asian American studies, Hyung-Chan Kim compiled the *Dictionary of Asian American History* in 1986 as a research resource on Asians in America.[50] An anthropologist, Priscilla Wegars, studied and collected early Asian immigrant material culture throughout the western United States in publications such as the 1993 *Hidden Heritage: Historical Archaeology of the Overseas Chinese*.[51] All of these underscore the body of scholarship on Asian American culture.

Is There a Pan-Asian Culture?

The presence of a pan-Asian culture in the United States is a topic of debate. According to some scholars, Asian American pan-ethnicity began with the administrative lumping of Asian ethnicities into one category. The rationale was based on an administrative convenience rather than a cultural or linguistic connection. However, the groups saw the political benefit of working together, culminating in the coining of the term "Asian American" in the 1960s.

Organizations and institutions have used the rubric of pan-Asianism as a political and economic rallying point in America, but Asian ethnic groups outside of the United States may not view themselves as a single bloc. The continued influx of new Asian groups tests the ability of the category to contain all those it claims to represent.

The distinction of "Asian" has been defined by the Federal Government for administrative purposes, such as census and other governmental records, and follows no particular pattern or known socio-political grouping.[52] The presumed commonalities among the various groups lie in physical characteristics and a rough geographic relation, not cultural bonds. There is no consistency even in this methodology. For example, although part of Asia, someone from Iran would have been considered white, rather than Asian, according to older census data. Now, the Middle East has its own category. Unlike Hispanic/Latino/Chicano Americans, who share many common cultural antecedents and may share a language or African Americans, many of whom share a common experience influenced by slavery and Jim Crow, the diversity of the Asian cultural experience in the United States creates difficulties in addressing these multiple ethnicities as a single entity.

The similarities within groups lie in the systematic estrangement of Asian ethnicities within American society. For decades, the battles for social justice in the United States have formed a common experience. Efforts to embrace the promise of America met with

> *The distinction of "Asian" has been defined by the Federal Government for administrative purposes, such as census and other governmental records, and follows no particular pattern or known socio-political grouping.*

the reality of exclusionary governmental policies. Asian Americans found themselves striving for rights and equality under the law, as individuals and as a group.

Continued and increased immigration of Asian ethnicities further alters the picture of pan-Asianism in America. The older native Asian communities have become more static, and more westernized. Fifth-generation Pinoy may not have the same concerns as the recent immigrant from the Philippines, for example.[53] The inherent differences between the various cultures become more pronounced, creating hybrid cultures that are constantly in flux. New Asian groups are incorporated into the greater Asian American population. Different Asian groups must develop relationships with one another and all of them must find a place of intersection with the greater American culture. The addition of each generation causes a redefining of Asian American culture.

An Asian American syncretism may be occurring. The latest census data indicate a large proportion of people of multiple Asian descents. Families blend heritages within the context of the ever-changing American culture. The global economy will only serve to encourage such melding. Hawaii, with its long-inclusive and blended society, represents the best example of pan-Asianism. However, its physical and cultural isolation from the contiguous United States marks it as an exception.

Conclusion

Asian groups have made and continue to make an impact on the landscape of America. The impact of Asian contributions to the built environment in America has yet to be appreciated in its fullness, for much has been lost and even more has yet to be studied in depth. The surface of the topic has only been scratched and more research into the resources needs to take place. Documentation of enclaves and a greater sensitivity to ephemeral culture is needed, not just for Asian ethnicities, but also for all of the nation's diverse communities.

The role of early immigrant groups cannot be overstated, but the rising demographic figures indicate that Asian American culture is on the verge of changing dramatically. This issue of continuous enrichment of cultures is being raised as communities continue the process of commemorating their histories. New research is available, but more attention should be paid to the varieties of Asian American cultures, how they can be represented in historic places, and how these places can benefit national preservation efforts overall.

ENDNOTES

1. There is a wealth of scholarship suggesting that people of Asian descent were the earliest arrivals in North America. These peoples migrated from Asia to North America over a prehistoric land bridge across the Bering Strait. Anthropological and genetic research indicates that three separate migrations from Asia may have taken place—the Amerind migration (before 10,000 B.C.), the Na-Dene migration (ca. 8,000 B.C.), and the Eskimo-Aleut migration (ca. 4,000 B.C.). Research also suggests that most North American Indians and all Indians of Central and South America are descendants from the first wave of migrants leaving Alaska after the Ice Age. Na-Dene migrants make up the coastal tribes of northwestern North America, such as the Tlingit and Haida. Apache and Navajo also descend from this migration. The Eskimo-Aleut migration settled the Arctic coastal regions with the ancestors of the modern Eskimo and Aleutian populations.

   This theory sits in contrast to several Indian traditions of a history on the North American continent dating back to time immemorial. For a sample of the information on the land bridge theory and alternate interpretations, see Ronald Carlisle, "Americans Before Columbus: Ice Age Origins", Ethnology Monographs 12, Department of Anthropology, University of Pittsburgh, 1988; A. L. Bryan, "New Evidence for the Pleistocene Peopling of the Americas," Center for the Study of Early Man, University of Maine, 1986; M. H. Crawford, *The Origins of Native Americans: Evidence from Anthropological Genetics* (Cambridge, UK and New York: Cambridge University Press, 1998).

2. Gavin Menzies postulates that ships of the Emperor Zhu Di circumnavigated the world from 1421-1423, arriving in the Americas 70 years before Columbus. During the 15th century, Chinese ships were sighted in ports of Eastern Africa and the Iberian Peninsula, which he cites as proof of the Chinese's technological ability. While evidence of this pre-Columbian contact needs further study, some scholars accept that the possibility exists, due to the nautical technology and knowledge of Chinese sailors of the era. Gavin Menzies, *1421: The Year China Discovered the World* (New York: William Morrow/HarperCollins, 2003); "The Year China Discovered America: A Roundtable Discussion," at the American Historical Association 118th Annual Meeting, Washington, DC, January 10, 2004; Louise Levathes, *When China Ruled the Seas* (Oxford, UK: Oxford University Press, 1996); and Michael L. Bosworth, "The Rise and Fall of 15th Century Chinese Seapower", from the Maritime History and Navigation Homepage, at http://www.cronab.demon.co.uk/marit.htm; accessed October 14, 2004.

3. Earlier dates can be attributed for Spanish contact with the Philippines. Ferdinand Magellan made landfall on Cebu island in 1521. Lopéz de Villalobos, traveling from New Spain (Mexico) named the islands for the infant king, Philip, in 1542. See "Philippines" at the Encyclopædia Britannica Premium Service at http://www.britannica.com/eb/article?tocId=23714; accessed October 11, 2004.

4. Eloisa Gomez Borah, "Filipinos in Unamuno's California Expedition" in *AMERASIA Journal* 21 no. 3(Winter 1996): 175-183.

5. See Jessica S. Barnes and Claudette E. Bennett, eds., *The Asian Population: US Census 2000 Brief* (Washington, DC: U.S. Department of Commerce, U.S. Census Bureau, 2002), 9, for a detailed listing of Asian groups enumerated in the United States.

6. See Barnes and Bennett, eds., *The Asian Population*, 8.

7. According to detailed census data found at the "Vietnamese Studies Internet Resource Center," at http://site.yahoo.com/vstudies/index.html; accessed September 25, 2003.

8. This increase is partially due to the revised methodology used by the Census Bureau, which allows for more flexible definitions of ethnicity. Barnes and Bennett, eds., *The Asian Population*, 3.

9. Barnes and Bennett, *The Asian Population*, 9.

10. Elizabeth M. Grieco, *Native Hawaiian and other Pacific Islander Population: US Census 2000 Brief* (Washington, DC: U.S. Department of Commerce, U.S. Census Bureau, 2003), 1.

11. The founding of the Manila Colony in St. Malo Bayou near New Orleans by Filipino sailors (a.k.a. Manila Men) has been a matter of academic discussion for some time, but most scholars put the date in the 1760s. This would make it the first Asian settlement in U.S. See

Fred Cordova's discussion with Marina Espina in *Filipinos: The Forgotten Asian Americans* (Seattle: Demonstration Project for Asian Americans, 1983), 1-7. Eloisa Gomez Borah has developed a website dedicated to Filipino history which refers to Espina and her discussions on the Manila Men and the colony. See further, "Americans of Filipino Descent FAQ" at http://personal.anderson.ucla.edu/eloisa.borah/filfaqs.htm#history, accessed November 20, 2003.

12. See William S. Bernard, "Immigration: the History of U.S. Policy," in *Harvard Encyclopedia of American Ethnic Groups*, ed. Stephen Thernstrom (Cambridge, MA: Belknap Press, 1980), 486-495, referenced in Luciano Mangiafico, *Contemporary American Immigrants: Patterns of Filipino, Korean, and Chinese Settlement in the United States* (New York: Praeger, 1988), 4, note 2.

13. Tabarah gives 1798 as the date of the first Chinese resident in Hawaii. See Ruth Tabrah, *Hawaii, A Bicentennial History* (New York [Nashville, TN]: W.W. Norton and Co. [American Association for State and Local History], 1980), 26. For the chronology of Asian history in Sucheng Chan, *Asian Americans: An Interpretative History.* Twayne's Immigrant History of America Series (New York: Twayne Publishers, 1991), 192-199.

14. 50,000 Chinese immigrants arrived in California in 1852 compared with 200 in Hawaii. See Chan, *Asian Americans*, 28.

15. The 1850 California Foreign Miners' Tax and other ordinances sought to eliminate the economic competition of Chinese miners. It also brought in a great deal of revenue to the state treasury. See Franklin Odo, ed., *The Columbia Documentary History of the Asian American Experience* (New York: Columbia University Press, 2002), 15.

16. For this and all other federal legislation referenced, see the "List of Federal Legislation Related to Asian Groups in the United States" in the appendix of the publication.

17. See Hilary F. Conroy, *The Japanese Frontier in Hawaii, 1868-1898* (Los Angeles and Berkeley: University Press of California, 1953), 15-43.

18. Japanese from certain prefectures were selected for their supposed agricultural acumen. See Isami Arifuku Waugh, Alex Yamato, and Raymond Y. Okamura, "The Japanese in California," in *Five Views: An Ethnic Historic Site Survey of California*, California Department of Parks and Recreation, Office of Historic Preservation, at http://www.cr.nps.gov/history/online_books/5views/5views.htm, accessed January 14, 2004.

19. Areas where the pre-World War II Japanese American population lived in San Francisco's Western Addition were destroyed to make way for the Geary Street Expressway. By 1960, 50 percent of the core of Japantown had been demolished. See *Nikkei Heritage* "San Francisco Japantown: the Prewar Era" 12, no. 3(Summer 2000); *Nikkei Heritage* "Redevelopment and Urban Japantowns" 13, no. 1(Fall/Winter 2000); and "Japantown Historic Context Statement, Landmarks Preservation Advisory Board, October 2003," 8.

20. Several sources for this date. See In-Jin Yoon, "Koreans" in *Asian American Encyclopedia*, Volume 3, ed. Franklin Ng (New York: Marshall Cavendish, 1995); Hyung-chan Kim, "Koreans" in *Harvard Encyclopedia of American Ethnic Groups*, ed. Stephen Thernstrom (Cambridge, MA: Belknap Press, 1980), 601; Yo-Jun Yun, "Early History of Korean Immigration to America" in *The Korean Diaspora*, ed. Hyung-chan Kim (Santa Barbara, CA: ABC-Clio, Inc., 1977), 33-45.

21. See Kim, "Koreans" in *Harvard Encyclopedia*, 604; Chan, *Asian Americans*, 15.

22. Several nations had imperial designs on Korea during the latter part of the 19th century. Japan began pressing Korea, which followed an isolationist policy similar to that of China, to develop a more advantageous political and economic relationship around 1868, as a part of Japan's more aggressive policy in the region. Japan's formal hegemony over Korea did not come to fruition until 1906, however by the early part of the 1900s, Japanese control was evident. Negotiations with the United States that led to the Gentlemen's Agreement of 1907, which prevented Japanese laborers from immigrating to the U.S., consequently applied to Korea. See Yun, "Early History," in *Korean Diaspora*, 37-38.

23. The War Brides Act of 1945 allowed Korean women to join their American military husbands in the United States. This began a trend of female-dominated Korean immigration to America. Between 1959 and 1971, 70 percent of Korean immigrants were female. See Odo, *Columbia Documentary*, 312-313; Kim, "Koreans," 606.

24. Reports dating to 1790 of a "Man from Madras" who stayed in Salem, Massachusetts, for roughly one year set the timeframe for an Asian Indian presence. The first Asian Indians were likely indentured servants of the British ship captains and traders prior to the 1790s. See Sucheta Mazumdar, "Asian Indians" in *Asian American Encyclopedia*, Volume 1, ed. Franklin Ng (New York: Marshall Cavendish, 1995), 93-94; and Vishnu Sharma, "A History of Indian Americans" at the Indian Community Center website, http://www.indiacc.org/site/Resources/Documents/article_ihd2004_sharma.pdf; accessed July 27, 2004.

25. The Asian Indian population grew from 491 in 1899 to 1.9 million as of the 2000 census. The highly skilled nature of much of the Asian Indian group in the U.S. is partially attributed to the "brain drain" phenomenon—the exportation of intellectual manpower from developing nations to the United States that coincided with 1965 amendment to the Immigration and Nationality Act. See Barnes and Bennett, *The Asian Population*, p. 9; Sharma, "A History of Indian Americans"; Parmatma Saran, *The Asian Indian Experience in the United States* (New Dehli, India: Vikas Press, 1985), 23.

26. Larry Salomon, "Movement History: Filipinos Build a Movement for Justice in the Asparagus Fields," in *Third Force* 2, no. 4(Oct. 31, 1994): 30. For more detailed discussion on Filipino labor unions, see Craig Scharlin and Linia V. Villanueva, *Philip Vera Cruz: A Personal History of Filipino Immigrants and the Farmworkers Movement* (Los Angeles: UCLA Labor Center and the UCLA Asian American Studies Center, 1992).

27. "Often, other Asians don't even consider Filipinos to be Asian," noted journalist Victor Merina. See "Aspects of Americanization: Victor Merina" in Joann Faung Jean Lee, *Asian American Experiences in the United States: Oral Histories of First to Fourth Generation Americans from China, the Philippines, Japan, India, the Pacific Islands, Viet Nam, and Cambodia* (Jefferson, NC: McFarland Press, 1991), 131.

28. The maritime trade related to Chinese hegemony, to include Japan, Korea and Malaysia, in the region predated European contact by hundreds of years. Yet, the story of the "discovery" of Pacific Islands begins with Magellan and ends with James Cook's arrival in Hawaii between 1772 and 1775. See Ron Adams, "European Discovery or Multiple Discoveries" in Max Quanchi and Ron Adams, eds. *Culture Contact in the Pacific: Essays on Contact, Encounter, and Response* (Cambridge, UK, and New York: Cambridge University Press, 1993), 31-37; Malama Meleisea and Penelope Schoffel, "Discovering Outsiders" in Donald Denoon, with Stewart Firth, Jocelyn Linnekin, Malama Meleisea, and Karen Nero, ed. *The Cambridge History of the Pacific Islands* (Cambridge, UK and New York: Cambridge University Press, 1997), 148-150.

29. Archeologically speaking, contact with the larger Pacific Islands began some 3,500 years ago, with travelers from Southeast Asia, more than likely from modern Taiwan, Malaysia, and Indonesia, to the Solomon Islands. Micronesia was settled between 2,000 and 2,500 years ago, and Hawaii, over 1,600 years ago. The Hawaiian and Samoan people are ancestors of Polynesian migrants to the islands. The Mariana Islands, which includes Guam and Saipan, is home to Chamorro culture, ancestors of those immigrants that settled the Solomon Islands. See Max Quanchi and Ron Adams, "Introduction" in *Culture Contact in the Pacific*, 8-10.

30. See "The Company Village," pamphlet (Vancouver, WA: Fort Vancouver National Historic Site, National Park Service, 2002); "The Village," brochure (Vancouver, WA: Fort Vancouver National Historic Site, National Park Service, 2002).

31. Statistics on Pacific Islander migration have only been kept since the 1980 census. See Bradd Shore, "Pacific Islanders" in *Harvard Encyclopedia of Ethnic Groups*, ed. Stephen Therstrom (Cambridge, MA: Belknap Press, 1980), 763-765.

32. See the discussion on the role of Christianity and Korean immigrants in Yun, "Early History"; Steven L. Austin, "The Role of Christianity in the Korean Migration to Hawaii, 1901-1913" (Ph.D. dissertation, University of Hawaii, 2000), 13-23.

33. The lack of documented presence of Asians in American culture reflects the "racialization" of Asian ethnicities within a binary racial system of white and black. In the racialization model, this binary opposition served to define who was "white" as much as who was not. Scholarship suggests that the existing paradigm did not deal as well with other people of color. Just as laws

were being amended to allow for the legal inclusion of African Americans, whose cultural impact by 1870 in the United States has been documented, if not agreed upon, Asian ethnicities found themselves further excluded from American culture. Asians were defined as "inassimilable," in addition to not being white or free, and could not become citizens. This idea and the subsequent actions taken against Asians and Asian Americans persisted until the middle of the 20th century, marginalizing Asian Americans and their culture, pushing them "out of sight" of the general public.

For discussions on racialization, see Michael Omi and Howard Winant, *Racial Formation in the United States: From the 1960s to the 1980s* (New York: Routledge Press, 1986). For more discussions on Asian Americans, race, and culture see Yen Le Espiritu, *Asian American Panethnicity: Bridging Institutions and Identities* (Philadelphia: Temple University Press, 1992), especially 172-173; Lisa Lowe, *Immigrant Acts: On Asian American Cultural Politics* (Durham, NC: Duke University Press, 1997), 1-59; Frank Wu, *Yellow: Race Beyond Black and White* (New York: Basic Books, 2001).

34. The various legislative actions against Asian groups are well documented. Asian immigrants were not allowed to become naturalized citizens of the United States. Since 1790, the criteria for admittance of Asian natives to the United States were much more restrictive than that for Anglo-European immigrants. Laws such as the 1924 National Origins Act, "set the parameters for desirable, less desirable, and undesirable ethnic and nationality groups," according to Franklin Odo in *Columbia Documentary History*. Asian nationalities fell into the undesirable category, as evinced by the 100 Asians per year allowed to immigrate into the United States. These quotas persisted until 1965. Only a small percentage of those persons allowed to immigrate were women, due to the 1875 Page Law, reportedly intended to curtail prostitution. Some states had laws against the ownership of property by Asians, prohibiting marriage with European Americans, and limiting where they could live.

Elaborate means, such as the creation of fictitious relatives or "paper families" were necessary to gain entrance. Prohibitions on owning property were circumvented by placing property in the names of American-born children when possible, or by secret arrangements with European Americans or other individuals. Odo, *Columbia Documentary History*, 128; see 12, 38 for reference to the Page Law; Chan, *Asian Americans*, 192-199.

35. See Yi-Fu Tuan, *Space and Place: The Perspective of Experience* (Minneapolis and London: University of Minnesota Press, 2001), 8-18; and Dolores Hayden, *The Power of Place: Urban Landscapes in Public History* (Cambridge, MA and London: MIT Press, 1995).

36. In examining place in Los Angeles, Dolores Hayden addresses the Japantown on First Street, noting the attachment of the greater Japanese community to the area despite demographic changes. It was transformed from Japanese American to African American (Bronzeville) back to Japanese American due to relocation to internment camps. See Hayden, *The Power of Place*, 210-225, 240-247.

37. The National Register criteria for listing are intended to be broad and inclusive, but as the types of properties and cultural attributes expand, the flexibility is being tested. See National Register Bulletin, "Guidelines for Evaluating and Documenting Traditional Cultural Properties" and "How to Apply the National Register Criteria for Evaluation;" see also Antoinette J. Lee, "Discovering Old Cultures in the New World: The Role of Ethnicity," in *The American Mosaic: Preserving A Nation's Heritage*, eds. Robert E. Stipe and Antoinette J. Lee (Washington, DC: Preservation Press, 1987), 180-205.

38. The Chinese sites at the Warren Historic Mining District in Idaho provide a physical record of Chinese immigrants and cultural practices in the American West. See National Register of Historic Places, *Chinese Sites in the Warren Mining District Multiple Property Survey, Idaho County, Idaho, National Register #1696100*. The Takahasi Farm represents the only archeological site associated with Japanese family farms studied in the state of California. See John Kelley, Judith Marvin, Christian Gerike, and Neal Kaptain, "Historic Property Survey Report (Positive) for the Sierra College Boulevard/ Interstate 80 Interchange Improvements, City of Rocklin Placer County, California," LSA Associates, Inc., Point Richmond, California, October 2002.

39. See Ned Kaufman, "Cultural Heritage Needs Assessment: Phase 1," draft, April 8, 2004, U.S. Department of the Interior, National Park Service; Hayden, *Power of Place*, 82-96.

40. Lisa Lowe argues that European Americans make a self-evident claim of citizenship, which had to be legally bestowed on the diverse peoples in the country. Prior to the Naturalization Act of 1790, citizenship was determined by the states. These laws evolved from British Colonial codes, specifically those of 1740 and 1761. See Lowe, *Immigrant Acts*, 11-14; Reed Ueda, " Naturalization and Citizenship," in *Harvard Encyclopedia of American Ethnic Groups*, ed. Stephen Thernstrom (Cambridge, MA: Belknap Press, 1980), 734-748.

41. See Sharma, "A History of Indian Americans"; Espina's study of Filipinos in the U.S., *Filipinos.*

42. Rose Hum Lee, *The Chinese in the United States of America* (Hong Kong: Hong Kong University Press, 1960).

43. Christopher Yip, "A Chinatown of Gold Mountain," in *Images of an American Land: Vernacular Architecture in the Western United States*, ed. Thomas Carter (Albuquerque: University of New Mexico Press, 1997), 153-172; "Chinese," in *America's Architectural Roots: Ethnic Groups that Built America*, ed. Dell Upton (Washington, DC: Preservation Press, 1986), 106-112.

44. Gail Dubrow with Donna Graves, *Sento at Sixth and Main: Preserving Landmarks of Japanese American Heritage* (Seattle: University of Washington Press, 2002).

45. Odo, *Columbia Documentary History.*

46. Mary Roberts Coolidge, *Chinese Immigration* (New York: Holt and Company, 1909).

47. Chan, *Asian Americans*; Sucheng Chan, *This Bittersweet Soil: The Chinese in California Agriculture, 1860-1910* (Los Angeles and Berkeley: University of California Press, 1991).

48. Him Mark Lai, *A History Reclaimed: An Annotated Bibliography of Chinese Language Materials on the Chinese of America* (Los Angeles: UCLA Asian American Studies Center, 1986).

49. Gary Okihiro, *The Columbia Guide to Asian American History* (New York: Columbia University Press, 2001).

50. Hyung-chan Kim, *Dictionary of Asian American History* (Westport, CT: Greenwood Publishing, 1986). See also his *Asian American Studies: An Annotated Bibliography and Research Guide* (Westport, CT: Greenwood Publishing, 1989).

51. Priscilla Wegars, ed., *Hidden Heritage: Historical Archaeology of the Overseas Chinese* (Amityville, NY: Baywood Publishing Company, 1993). Wegars is curator of the Asian American Comparative Collection, housed in the Laboratory of Anthropology at University of Idaho, Moscow. See Priscilla Wegars, "Chinese Artifact Illustrations, Terminology, and Selected Bibliography," prepared for the Chinese and Japanese Workshop, Society for Historical Archaeology, Salt Lake City, UT, January 1999; "Japanese Artifact Illustrations, Terminology, and Selected Bibliography," prepared for the Chinese and Japanese Workshop, Society for Historical Archaeology, Salt Lake City, UT, January 1999.

52. This approach is consistent with similar attempts to homogenize other multiple ethnicities into large, single racial groups, such as sub-Saharan Africans and various Hispanics/Latinos. The Office of Management and Budget's Directive Number 15 on Race and Ethnic Standards spells out the federal process. A report on the usage of the directive has since been undertaken and the results led to the recent revamping of census data collection methods to allow for multiple listings under the "race" and "ethnicity" categories. See Espiritu, *Asian American Panethnicity*, 13; Office of Management and Budget "Race and Ethnic Standards for Federal Statistics and Administrative Reporting,"(May 12, 1977); and Interagency Committee for the Review of Racial and Ethnic Standards, "Report to the Office of Management and Budget on Statistical Policy Directive Number 15," memorandum (May 28, 1997).

53. See discussion of heterogeneity of Asian American culture and the need to recognize it in "Heterogeneity, Hybridity and Multiplicity: Asian American Differences," in Lowe, *Immigrant Acts*, 60-83. Yen Le Espiritu discusses the dominance of older communities in the formation of a pan-Asian identity; see Espiritu, *Asian American Panethnicity*, 50-52.

Identifying and Documenting Asian Heritage on the American Landscape

Through its cultural resources programs, the National Park Service has identified and formally recognized historic places associated with Asian cultural heritage. Historic places having a connection with Asian heritage have been listed in the National Register of Historic Places, designated as National Historic Landmarks, documented through the Historic American Buildings Survey/Historic American Engineering Record, and identified through theme studies, such as "Racial Desegregation in Public Education in the United States." This chapter highlights several examples of such historic places and summarizes their connection to Asian cultures.

The properties that have been recognized by National Park Service cultural resources programs include:

- those that are representative of ethnic heritage, as in the case of the Stedman-Thomas Historic District in Ketchikan, Alaska
- embody distinctive physical characteristics, such as Wakamiya Inari Shrine in Honolulu, Hawaii
- those that are associated with events and persons that have made significant contributions to the broad patterns of our history, such as the Presidio of San Francisco, California
- those that may yield or are likely to yield information important in early history or history, such as Leluh Ruins in Kosrae, Micronesia.

The discussion suggests the types of historic places that communities might consider for formal documentation and recognition.

National Register of Historic Places

The National Register of Historic Places is the nation's inventory of historic districts, sites, buildings, structures, and objects significant in American history, architecture, archeology, engineering, and culture at the national, state, and local levels. The National Register contains nearly 78,000 properties and with over 1 million historic resources within those properties.

Jun Fujita Cabin

International Falls, Minnesota

Located in Voyageurs National Park, on an island at Rainy Lake, the Jun Fujita Cabin illuminates several aspects of the Asian experience in America. Fujita was a photographer, artist, and poet, who immigrated from Japan to Canada during his late teens. The young Fujita found work as a photographer with the *Chicago Evening Post* (which later was absorbed into the *Chicago Evening News* in the 1930s) in 1915. He photographed celebrated figures, such as presidents Woodrow Wilson, Herbert Hoover, and Theodore Roosevelt; Al Capone; and Clarence Darrow. He covered famous events such as the sinking of the USS *Eastland* in the Chicago River in 1915. Later, he devoted himself to artistic endeavors as a photographer and painter. Fujita gained fame in the 1920s as a poet, writing in haiku and tanka forms.[1]

During the late 1920s, he either commissioned or constructed the cabin in International Falls. From 1928 to 1941, Fujita used the cabin as a place of relaxation and reflection, which may have been an influence on his art. At the time, less than five percent of the Asian population in the country lived outside of Hawaii and the West Coast.

The National Register documentation describes the Fujita Cabin as a frame cabin of unfinished cedar, with two log additions—a log room with a hipped roof and a shed porch. While the construction of the original cabin in 1928 comports with typical recreational cabin design, the additions exhibit Japanese influences. The log room is narrow, and the floor is elevated.[2] The setting of the cabin, natural materials, simple lines, and light construction reflect Japanese country house design. This organic architectural form blends the cabin into the surrounding landscape. Descriptions of Japanese architecture contemporaneous with Fujita's arrival in North America describe a similar aesthetic.[3]

■ The Jun Fujita cabin combines the aesthetics of Japanese country house design with western log cabin construction to create a naturalistic structure with minimal impact on its environment.

Courtesy of John Hurley

Although Japanese immigration was restricted by 1908, working as a photographer allowed Fujita to enter the United States. Despite his success, the nation's discriminatory laws and practices haunted Fujita. His wife, Florence Carr, bought the four-acre island in Minnesota in her name, it is believed, because of fears it might be confiscated due to laws restricting land ownership by aliens.[4] Although he avoided internment because of his residence in Chicago, Fujita abandoned the property after the United States entered World War II in 1941 and anti-Japanese sentiments increased, preferring to use another vacation property in Indiana from 1941 onward.[5] By a special act of Congress in 1954, Fujita was granted United States citizenship. His cabin reflects Japanese influence on the built environment.

Wakamiya Inari Shrine
Honolulu, Hawaii
One of the few examples of authentic Shinto architecture on Oahu, the shrine represents Japanese cultural practices. Shinto is a native Japanese religion, which venerates natural objects and ancestors. Polytheistic in nature, the faith has a pantheon of figures, but four are predominant: Hachimangu, Tenjin, Jinju, and Inari. The Wakamiya Shrine is devoted to Inari, the god of the harvest, and is especially related to fields of production, such as agriculture. It is called the fox deity, because foxes are thought to be messengers for Inari.

■ The Wakamiya Shrine is the only extant temple dedicated to Inari on the island of Oahu, HI. The shrine exhibits the major components of Inari temple design, including an archway to demarcate sacred space and protective animistic statuary.

Courtesy of Nancy Bannick

According to the National Register documentation, the shrine is representative of Shinto architecture because it exhibits the traditional statuary (protective lions in the courtyard and foxes in front of the shrine) and the *torii*, an archway used to demarcate the sacred place being entered. Built in 1914 by Japanese architect Haschun, under the direction of Reverend Yoshio Akizaki, for the community of agricultural workers, it is the only example of an Inari shrine on the island. The shrine has been moved twice, most recently to Waipahu Cultural Garden in 1979-1980.[6] It was one of the last places of worship for members of the Inari sect in Oahu.

Stedman-Thomas Historic District
Ketchikan Gateway Borough, Alaska

Economically significant as a supplier and processor of salmon and halibut, the Stedman-Thomas Historic District was home to Japanese, Chinese, Korean, and Filipino communities involved in the city's fishing industry from the 1900s to the 1940s. Located in the southern section known as Indian Town, Stedman-Thomas represents a place of diaspora for Asian groups during the early 20th century. The vast majority of Ketchikan's diverse communities lived in the historic district. Asian and other minority laborers migrated north to Alaska to work in the canneries and fisheries. Many of the first businesses, including restaurants, hotels, and grocery stores, were owned and operated by Asian families, such as [George] Ohashi's Grocery, the Japanese school, and Jimmy's [Tanino] Noodles. Despite the segregated nature of the community, the Asian community of Stedman-Thomas found a degree of freedom in commercial and organizational endeavors.[7]

> *The district maintains a high degree of integrity and includes two-story, flat front buildings, with some false fronts, many of which date to the early 1900s.*

When Federal laws restricted the immigration of the Chinese and Japanese during the 1920s, Filipinos were recruited to work in Ketchikan canneries. As a result, Ketchikan had one of the earliest permanent Filipino communities in Alaska, as well as the state's first Filipino social organization, the Filipino Social Club.[8] During the 1940s, the ethnic composition of Stedman-Thomas changed and its business backbone was broken when 42 people of Japanese descent were forced into internment camps. Many of them did not return. The dissolution of the Japanese community coincided with the decline of the Alaskan fishing industry. Many of the businesses that depended on the patronage of fishermen fell upon hard times. Eventually, lumbering replaced fishing as the primary industry.

The district maintains a high degree of integrity and includes two-story, flat front buildings, with some false fronts, many of which date to the early 1900s. The neighborhood is still diverse and shared by Asian groups. Named for one of the Japanese families that owned a grocery, Tatsuda Way runs through the district. The Stedman-Thomas Historic District is a significant historic place that represents Asian ethnic heritage in North America during the early 20ᵗʰ century.

Leluh Ruins
Kosrae County, Federated States of Micronesia
The Leluh Ruins are significant as a site associated with the Kosraen society, an early society that developed into a "state" system around A.D. 1400. Made up of tall basalt and coral walls and several types of structures, the site represents the center of Kosrae power until European contact in 1824.

Leluh Ruins is identified as the capital of the prehistoric Kosrae society.[9] It was an independent nation of 42 square miles and 6,000 people located on Korsae Island and the three nearby islets of Pisin, Yensar, and Yenyen. The site is noteworthy for the massive walls of basalt prisms and blocks that surround the compounds. At least 100 structures of 3 different types—dwellings, royal mortuary, and sacred—are present. Because of the distinctive architecture and the canal system, the site is referred to as a "Wonder of the Pacific." The Leluh Ruins may hold significant information about the religious practices and the social structure of the Kosrae population prior to European contact.

National Historic Landmarks
Designated by the Secretary of the Interior, National Historic Landmarks are nationally significant historic places because they possess exceptional value or quality in illustrating or interpreting the heritage of the United States. Approximately 2,500 historic places bear this distinction.

Because of the distinctive architecture and the canal system, the site is referred to as a "Wonder of the Pacific." The Leluh Ruins may hold significant information about the religious practices and the social structure of the Kosrae population prior to European contact.

Japanese American World War II Theme Study

In 1991, Congress authorized the National Park Service to prepare a National Historic Landmark Theme Study on 37 sites associated with the Japanese American experience during the period from 1941 to 1946. In response to the Japanese attack on Pearl Harbor and the subsequent United States involvement in World War II, Japanese aliens and Japanese American citizens were ordered detained, relocated, or excluded. The purpose of the study is to identify historic places that exemplify and illustrate the period. The following discussion presents examples of properties associated with the theme study.

The Presidio of San Francisco, Buildings 35 and 640
San Francisco, California

Established in 1776 as a Spanish colonial military post, the Presidio of San Francisco is the oldest Army installation in the western United States and one of the longest-garrisoned posts in the country. Its development is tied to the Spanish colonial rule in northern Mexico (the present-day American Southwest and West Coast) and to every major conflict since the Mexican-American War. Two of the more than 660 contributing resources hold particular significance to Asian Americans, Buildings 35 and 640.

Building 35 was the site where President Franklin D. Roosevelt issued Executive Order 9066 on February 19, 1942, which placed the West Coast under military authority. An enlisted men's barracks and mess hall, the building also served as the headquarters for the Western Defense Command (WDC), the United States Fourth Army command responsible for the removal of over 100,000 persons of Japanese descent from the restricted areas of the West Coast.[10] From this location, General John L. DeWitt directed the evacuation of Japanese and Japanese Americans to relocation and detention centers far removed from the coast, in places ranging from Idaho to Arkansas.

The executive order and subsequent actions were a continuation of federal policy towards Asians in America and indicative of public sentiment, particularly in the West.[11] The actions of the Federal Government caused irreparable damage to Japanese American culture. Gail Dubrow noted, "The closure of community institutions such as *dojo*, temples, and language schools, and the wholesale evacuation of Japanese American communities, disassembled Japanese American heritage and unjustly deprived innocent people of their freedom."[12]

"The closure of community institutions such as dojo, *temples, and language schools, and the wholesale evacuation of Japanese American communities, disassembled Japanese American heritage and unjustly deprived innocent people of their freedom."*

■ During World War II, a high premium was placed on the ability to read and speak Japanese. The Presidio Language School, or Building 640 as it was officially known, trained military intelligence officers in Japanese. Some of the instructors, shown in 1944, were second-generation Japanese Americans or *nisei*.

Courtesy of the Golden Gate National Recreation Area

A former airplane hangar at Crissy Field, Building 640 served as the classrooms for the Military Intelligence Service Language School (MISLS) or Fourth Army Intelligence School, where military intelligence service and civilian Japanese American personnel taught the Japanese language to selected soldiers, primarily those of Japanese descent born in America (also known as *nisei*). Prior to the outbreak of hostilities with Japan, the Army began secretly recruiting and assembling some 60 soldiers or linguists. By early 1942, 35 MISLS graduates were trained and ready for deployment. Some 2,000 MISLS linguists served with distinction throughout the Pacific theater.[13]

According to the theme study, Building 640 housed classrooms and barracks for the initial MISLS participants. The program began in November 1941 at the Presidio, but was moved to Fort Savage and eventually to Fort Snelling in Minnesota. Ostensibly, the move was made to provide larger, better facilities. However, the anti-Japanese sentiment prevalent in California played a part. Eventually the program returned to California, to the Presidio of Monterey, and the program was renamed the Defense Language Institute.

Buildings 35 and 640 of the Presidio of San Francisco exemplify the duality of the Asian experience—the discriminatory treatment of an Asian ethnicity juxtaposed against the group's service to the nation's defense.

Racial Desegregation in Public Education in the United States Theme Study

In 1998, Congress authorized the National Park Service to prepare a National Historic Landmark Theme Study on racial desegregation in public education. As defined by the legislation authorizing the theme, it addresses the events that surround public school segregation and the eventual desegregation. Properties identified in the theme study are associated with these events. The following is an example of a property associated with the theme study

Rosedale Consolidated High School
Rosedale, Mississippi

Gong Lum, a Chinese grocer in Bolivar County, Mississippi, enrolled his oldest daughter Martha, at the local white Rosedale Consolidated High School. In 1924, the superintendent informed Lum that his daughter could no longer attend the school because she was not white. The school system was segregated under the "separate but equal" ruling handed down in the 1896 landmark case *Plessy v. Ferguson*, which allowed for the constitutionality of state segregation laws during the Jim Crow era.[14] The "colored" schools had inferior equipment, teachers, and dramatically shorter school years. Lum sued the school in the United States Circuit Court, First Judicial District, on behalf of his daughter and a school friend, Chew How. Lum's lawyers argued successfully that his daughter was not a "member of the colored race" and since there were no schools for Chinese, she was being denied an equal education and therefore entitled to attend the Rosedale School.

After being overturned by the Mississippi State Supreme Court, *Gong Lum, et al v. Rice, et al* eventually made it to the United States Supreme Court in 1927, where it was determined that the state intended to preserve white schools for white students alone, upholding the state's high court verdict. However, recognizing that such a practice violated the Fourteenth Amendment, also ruled that Chinese who were domestically-born, and therefore citizens, were granted the same privileges as African American citizens, tying Chinese Americans to Jim Crow segregation in Mississippi.[15] The Supreme Court directed Martha Lum to attend the colored school in the county or any private school of her choice. The first school for Chinese students in Rosedale was a Baptist Mission school that opened in 1934. White schools would not legally become available to Chinese students until 1950.[16]

The first school for Chinese students in Rosedale was a Baptist Mission school that opened in 1934. White schools would not legally become available to Chinese students until 1950.

The issue of education was one of the obstacles Chinese immigrants encountered as a third element in a biracial world. Chinese immigrants arrived in Mississippi during Reconstruction (1865-1877), recruited to fill the role of cheap agricultural laborers left by the emancipation of African Americans. Like their fellow countrymen in California, many hoped to earn a fortune and return home. Some quickly recognized that the sharecropping system in the South, tied to racial inequality, would not produce the desired effect of their labors and began opening grocery stores throughout the state. The earliest stores may have appeared as early as the 1870s, and Chinese are listed as landowners in Bolivar County in 1880s tax records.[17] Chinese merchants wanted the same opportunities as European Americans, while fiscally tied to the fortunes of the economically downtrodden, who where overwhelmingly black. By the time of the lawsuit, there were a few hundred Chinese students like Lum's daughter in all of the state. Their position in the South left them on the edges of the segregated society, but Chinese Americans "carved out a distinctive spot as a third element in a predominantly biracial society."[18]

Historic American Buildings Survey

The Historic American Buildings Survey (HABS) documents important architectural sites throughout the United States and its territories. The program is an integral component of the Federal Government's commitment to historic preservation. HABS documentation, consisting of measured drawings, large-format photographs, and written history, plays a key role in accomplishing the mission of creating an archive of American architecture and engineering, and in better understanding what historic resources tell us about America's diverse ethnic and cultural heritage.

Chinese Community Church
Washington, District of Columbia
The Chinese community in the District of Columbia dates back to the beginning of the 20th century. The Chinatown community was displaced from its original location on Pennsylvania Avenue near 4th Street, NW, by the construction of what became known as Federal Triangle in the 1920s and 1930s. The community resettled north to H Street, NW, and established new organizations and institutions in extant commercial buildings and residential housing. By the 1930s, several churches had organized Chinese Sunday

■ The Chinese Community Church of Washington, DC, employed Chinese design motifs in its architecture to connect the building to the community's cultural antecedents. This 1974 photograph shows the building's ornate parapet and entranceway.

Photograph by Jack E. Boucher, courtesy of the Historic American Building Survey

School classes. Dr. Pak-Chue Chan, a medical director at George Washington University, envisioned a Chinese church in the District, and cooperated with the DC Federation of Churches and others to establish one. In 1935, the Chinese Community Church of Washington, DC, was incorporated and constructed on the lot at 1011 L Street, NW in 1939. In 1957, the first service was held at the church.[19]

A brick structure with a recessed entranceway and limestone trim, the building served as a church from 1957 until 1994. According to the Historic American Building Survey documentation, Chinese design motifs are incorporated into the ecclesiastical detailing, and the entranceway mullions are arranged in a Chinese openwork pattern.[20]

The Chinese Community Church has been a touchstone of the Chinatown community. The building housed the first all-Chinese Boy Scout troop and a Chinese language school, and was home to various clubs. Through the Chinatown Service Center, it provided a place for new immigrants to gain an introduction to the community and American culture. The church sponsored other outreach programs, helping hundreds of Asian immigrants each year.[21]

After 1994, the congregation outgrew the space, and currently shares a ministry with nearby Mount Vernon Episcopal. The church building serves as administrative offices for the congregation. The Chinese Community Church remains a place of cultural significance for Chinese Americans and the larger Asian American community in the Washington, DC, metropolitan area.

■ The Chinese Community Church served many functions in Washington, DC's Chinese community. Among them was as headquarters for the city's all-Chinese American Boy Scout troop, pictured in 1942.

Courtesy of the Chinese Community Church of Washington, DC

■ Locke still contains many of the original buildings from its founding in 1915. Some of the wood-frame structures bear Chinese calligraphic symbols and signage from the businesses that lined the streets. Other places such as the Joe Shoong Chinese School have been rehabilitated, while retaining their historic character.

Drawing by the Historic American Buildings Survey; photograph by Jet Lowe, courtesy of the Historic American Buildings Survey

Town of Locke
Locke, California

The town of Locke is the largest and most complete example of a rural Chinese American community in the United States. In 1915, merchants and laborers from the Chungshan and Sze Yap districts in Guangdong province founded the small town of Locke after a fire destroyed their homes in nearby Walnut Grove. A committee of six men secured a verbal lease from the landowner, the George Locke family, because anti-Asian legislation prevented the community from buying land. Nine acres of peach orchard were cleared and within a year, Locke was built.

Locke's original population was made up of agricultural laborers working the Sacramento-San Joaquin River Valley delta. Chinese workers made up 90 percent of all agricultural labor in California at the beginning of the 20th century.[22] Initially, Chinese laborers worked in the pear, apple, peach, and cherry orchards, in addition to potato and onion patches in the valley, until the asparagus boom around 1900. Afterwards, most of the land in the area was planted with asparagus. This boom, and the subsequent development of an asparagus canning industry, coincided with the rise of Locke.[23]

While most Chinese communities are urban enclaves, Locke is unique within the United States as the only surviving rural Chinese community still occupied by Chinese people. The town is made up of simple, wooden frame structures, built on concrete foundations and covered with clapboard or board-and-batten siding. The buildings are one- to two-stories high with gable roofs covered in corrugated metal or false fronts, housed stores, schools, and residences. Some of the facades bear Chinese motifs and signage with Chinese calligraphy. The Historic American Buildings Survey documented 191 structures in Locke.

Historic American Engineering Record

The Historic American Engineering Record (HAER) documents important engineering and industrial sites throughout the United States and its territories. The program is an integral component of the Federal Government's commitment to historic preservation. HAER documentation, consisting of measured drawings, large-format photographs, and written history, plays a key role in accomplishing the mission of creating an archive of American architecture and engineering, and in better understanding what historic resources tell us about America's diverse ethnic and cultural heritage.

Hanalei Pier

Kauai, Hawaii

By 1900, Hawaii was the third-leading producer of rice in the United States. Rice was Hawaii's second leading crop, behind sugar cane. Hanalei and Waioli were the largest rice-producing areas in Hawaii. Due to the location of the Hawaiian Islands in the Pacific Ocean, transportation played an important role in all agricultural production. The Hanalei Pier was used to transport rice grown and processed in the Hanalei Valley to Honolulu and to the mainland. It is one of the few remaining vestiges of the once-thriving rice industry in Hanalei.

Because of its scenic location in the Hanalei Bay, the pier has been featured in several movies, most notably South Pacific.

Chinese, and later Japanese, farmers found ready markets for rice in Honolulu and on the mainland, and helped make it Hawaii's second largest crop by 1892.[24] Hanalei Pier connects Asians and their influence on the built environment in Hawaii to the greater development of the United States' agricultural economy. The Hanalei Pier is an example of a typical finger pier in Hawaii during the 1920s. Originally built in 1892 as a short pier, it was reconstructed and extended in 1912, and a concrete deck was added in 1922. It served as a center for interisland transportation until 1933, when it was abandoned in favor of Nawiliwili harbor, on the southeast side of the island. Subsequently, Hanalei Pier became a recreational resource for locals for fishing and picnicking. Because of its scenic location in the Hanalei Bay, the pier has been featured in several movies, most notably *South Pacific*.

Conclusion

The historic preservation field has taken initial steps to recognize and record the influence of Asian groups on the American cultural landscape. Recent research highlights the variety of locations where Asian heritage have contributed to the American cultural landscape. The range of properties can be expanded to include places where other historic events took place. The role of Asians in the history of the South, for example, is an important theme that warrants further study.

A site or building does not need to bear the outward markings of an ethnic group to be significantly influenced by a group. The impact upon the local culture is important and can leave an impression beyond that of a building's form. The Stedman-Thomas Historic District receives over 500,000 visitors each year, due in part to the impact of the Asian immigrants who developed the city into an urban center in the wilderness. Similarly, the effects of Executive Order 9066 and the Language School at the Presidio cannot be discerned from the styles of the buildings. Applying the same approach to sites of legal battles over citizenship, labor activism, and desegregation of public education, a myriad of new places are open to identification.

A site or building does not need to bear the outward markings of an ethnic group to be significantly influenced by a group. The impact upon the local culture is important and can leave an impression beyond that of a building's form.

ENDNOTES

1. Haiku is an unrhymed verse form of three lines containing 17 syllables (5, 7, 5), while tanka, a similar form with five lines, contains 31 syllables (5, 7, 5, 7, 7) Fujita had poems published in several magazines, and published a collection of poems in 1923. See Jun Fujita, *Tanka: Poems in Exile* (Chicago: Covici-McGee, 1923).

2. One informant's description states the room contained two sleeping mats. The current occupant believes it was used as a shrine. See National Register of Historic Places, *Jun Fujita Cabin, St. Louis County, Minnesota. National Register #96001351.*

3. The National Register nomination cites the book by Edward S. Morse, *Japanese Homes and Their Surroundings* (New York: Dover Publications, 1961) for its evaluation of Japanese housing. Clay Lancaster surveyed the Japanese cultural impact in *The Japanese Influence in America* (New York: Walton H. Rawls, 1963) and examined the application of Japanese design in material culture as well as the built environment and drew similar conclusions about the design aesthetic.

4. Carr and Fujita owned property in several different states, including a vacation property in Indiana. See *Fujita Cabin, #96001315.*

5. Once the war commenced, the long trip from Chicago and the animosity toward Japanese Americans outweighed Fujita's desire for solitude. For example, Fujita's presence caused the locals to name the island, pejoratively, Jap Island. See *Fujita Cabin, #96001315.*

6. The issue of moving buildings and the maintenance of its integrity was considered and it was decided that the shrine maintained its integrity in the relocation. See National Register of Historic Places, *Wakamiya Inari Shrine, Honolulu County, Hawaii. National Register #80001285.*

7. See National Register of Historic Places, *Stedman-Thomas Historic District, Ketchikan Gateway, Alaska. National Register #96000062;* and "A Multicultural Melting Pot in Ketchikan, Alaska," in *CRM: Diversity and Cultural Resources* 22, no. 8(1999): 27.

8. *Stedman-Thomas Historic District, #96000062.*

9. The National Register nomination notes the significance of the political development of the Kosrae to the Pacific Islands. National Register of Historic Places, *Leluh Ruins, Kosrae Freely Associated State, Federated States of Micronesia. National Register #83004524.*

10. See *Japanese Americans in World War II: National Historic Landmark Theme Study* (Washington, DC: U.S. Department of the Interior, National Park Service, 2002), 1, 42; and National Historic Landmark Survey, *Presidio of San Francisco, San Francisco, San Francisco County, California.*

11. For a summary of the historiography of the Japanese American internment and the reasons for it, see Gary Y. Okihiro, *The Columbia Guide to Asian American History* (New York: Columbia University Press, 2001), 100-127. The book's discussion, "America's Concentration Camps," summarizes scholarship on the topic and books of interest.

12. Gail Dubrow, with Donna Graves, *Sento at Sixth and Main: Preserving Landmarks of Japanese American Heritage* (Seattle: University of Washington Press, 2002), 4.

13. James C. McNaughton, "Nisei Linguists and New Perspectives on the Pacific War: Intelligence, Race, and Continuity," paper presented at the Conference of Army Historians, 1994; National Japanese Historical Society, "Japanese Americans in the Military Intelligence Service" website at, http://www.njahs.org/misnorcal/index.htm; accessed January 5, 2004.

14. *Plessy v. Ferguson* and its effect is discussed at length in the theme study, *Racial Desegregation in Public Education in the US: National Historic Landmark Theme Study* (Washington, DC: U.S. Department of the Interior, National Park Service, 2002), 31, 33-40.

15. Sucheng Chan, *Asian Americans: An Interpretive History*, Twayne's Immigrant History of America Series (New York: Twayne Publishing, 1991), 58; and Franklin Odo, ed., *The Columbia Documentary History of the Asian American Experience* (New York: Columbia University Press, 2002), 211-214.

16. Sieglinde Lim de Sanchez, "Crafting a Delta Chinese Community: Education and Acculturation in Twentieth-Century Southern Baptist Mission Schools," *History of Education Quarterly* (Spring 2003), at http://www.historycooperative.org/journals/heq/43.1/sanchez.html; accessed March 25, 2004.

17. The majority of Chinese in the United States at the time were from Sze Yap, a district in southern China, which was a commercial center. See Charles Reagan Wilson, "Mississippi Chinese: An Ethnic People in a Biracial Society," *Mississippi History Now: An Online Publication*, at the Mississippi Historical Society website, posted November 2002 at http://mshistory.k12.ms.us/features/feature33/chinese.html; accessed on December 16, 2002 and January 5, 2004.

18. Wilson, "Mississippi Chinese."

19. See S.Y. Lueng, ed., *The Chinese Community Church 50th Anniversary Yearbook, 1935-1985* (Washington, DC: n.p., 1985), 103-104, 110.

20. See Historic American Buildings Survey, *Chinese Community Church, Washington, District of Columbia. HABS No. DC-281.*

21. See Lueng, *The Chinese Community Church 50ᵗʰ Anniversary Yearbook*, 119-121; The City Museum of Washington, DC, *Chinatown: People or Place?* exhibition manuscript, September 17, 2003.

22. The contribution of the Chinese to the development of the Sacramento-San Joaquin River delta cannot be overstated. In addition to agricultural production, Chinese labor dredged the swamps by building levees to create arable land. See Historic American Buildings Survey, *Town of Locke, Sacramento County, California. HABS No. CA-2071*; Dean E. Murphy, "This Land is Made, Finally, for Chinese Settlers," in *New York Times*, June 29, 2003, 17-20.

23. Historic American Buildings Survey, *Town of Locke, CA-2071.*

24. Chinese immigrants began growing rice in Hawaii around the mid-1800s. After the end of their contracts on sugar plantations, Chinese workers acquired taro patches and converted them into rice paddies. Japanese laborers who replaced the Chinese eventually took over the rice industry. However, rice production diminished due to the annexation of Hawaii by the United States in 1898, which extended the Federal exclusion policy of Chinese to the islands area and reduced the number of consumers. Another factor was the subsequent lifting of all tariffs that created a boom in the sugar market, encouraging farmers to convert rice fields more to the profitable sugar cane. Finally, an increase in rice production in California signaled the end of rice's heyday in Hawaii. See John Wesley Coulter and Chee Kwon Chen, "Chinese Rice Farmers in Hawaii," in *University of Hawaii Bulletin* 16, no. 5(1937): 18-22; and Historic American Engineering Record, *Hanalei Pier. HAER No. HI-17*; National Register of Historic Places, *Hanalei Pier, Kauai County, Hawaii. National Register #79000757.*

Interpreting Asian Heritage at Historic Sites

Interpretive programs that focus on Asian heritage present the many images of the Asian experience in the United States. While the western United States provides the most likely places for interpretative opportunities, places like Massachusetts are areas of interest because of recent immigration patterns.

Historic sites of difficult histories and the struggle for social justice provide opportunities to include Asian ethnic heritage as part of the interpretation. Newer Asian communities, such as the Vietnamese, Thai, Hmong, and Cambodian, are imprinting their cultures on communities and places. Many are using historic sites as cultural resources and are presenting interpretation opportunities for historic preservation managers. By addressing these recent issues within the interpretative framework of existing historic sites, Asian American heritage gains visibility and connects Asian Americans to the larger American story.

Lowell Historic Preservation District
Lowell, Massachusetts
The town of Lowell, Massachusetts, is associated with the Industrial Revolution in the United States. The spinning mills and mill buildings embody the rapid industrialization and urbanization of the country during the 1800s. By housing all of the facets of cloth production under one roof, from recruitment to production, the Waltham-Lowell system revolutionized textile manufacturing. Lowell was not only a textile giant, but it also produced tools for the textile mills, housed textile manufacturing shops, and built steam locomotives for the emerging New England rail system.

Lowell, and its surrounding neighborhoods, has been home to many different ethnic communities—Irish, French-Canadians, Portuguese, Poles, Russian Jews, Greeks, and more recently Latinos. In addition to these groups is an emerging Cambodian American community. After the passage of the Indochina Migration and Refugee Assistance Act of 1975, Cambodian refugees immigrated to the Boston area and to Lowell.[1] As of the 2000

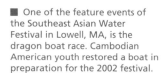

The Angkor Dance Troupe serves as a keeper of Cambodian culture for Khmer youth growing up in the United States. They learn traditional dances and wear traditional clothes, as the younger members of the troupe did at the Lowell Folk Festival in July 2001.

Courtesy of Kevin Harkins

census, the Cambodian American community accounted for over 17,000 people, or 20 percent of the population of Lowell. The community is concentrated around two areas known respectively as the Acre and the Highlands, both of which fall within the Lowell Historic District.

The Cambodian community has become an active part of the community-at-large, with the development of several civic institutions and participation in the annual Lowell Folk Festival.[2] In addition, the annual Southeast Asian Water Festival offers Cambodian, Vietnamese, and Laotian residents an opportunity to celebrate water as the source of life, with dragon boat races on the Merrimack River.[3] Lowell National Historic Park employees have taken a particular interest in the community, becoming involved with Cambodian American organizations, creating programs for the community at the park, and even visiting Cambodia to develop a better understanding of that culture. Cambodian Americans strive to keep their cultural heritage alive through the Angkor Dance Troupe housed in the Patrick J. Mogan Cultural Center at Lowell National Park. The troupe teaches folk and classical dance to local youth and enhances the appreciation of their heritage. Thus, the historic district incorporates Cambodian culture into its multicultural heritage.

One of the feature events of the Southeast Asian Water Festival in Lowell, MA, is the dragon boat race. Cambodian American youth restored a boat in preparation for the 2002 festival.

Courtesy of Joshua Reynolds

Chinese Sites in the Warren Mining District
Warren, Idaho

The desire for gold led many people to the American West and to Idaho. Chinese immigrants came by the thousands, hoping to become rich through mining. Sources indicate that Chinese made up the largest ethnic group in the state during Idaho's early settlement period.[4] The early mines were placer mines—loose mineral deposits near the surface found through panning in water. Some fortunes were made, but by the time the Warren miners voted to allow the Chinese to have mining rights in 1869, most of the easily obtained gold was gone. Despite this difficulty, a sizable Chinese community developed in Warren between 1870 and the 1890s. These laborers sought to maintain their traditional diet and lifeways as much as possible while in America. In addition to mining, they cultivated terraced gardens and opened shops that catered to the tastes of the community and provided services for the bachelor society in Warren.

Several National Register properties on China Mountain associated with Chinese heritage in the United States make up the Chinese Sites in the Warren Mining District Multiple Property Submission (MPS). These interrelated sites, Ah Toy Garden, Celadon Slope Garden, and Chi-Sandra Garden; Old China Trail; the Chinese Cemetery; and the Chinese Mining Camp Archeological Site, located in the Payette National Forest, tell the story of the Chinese experience in the West within the larger historic context of American westward expansion.

Because of the isolated nature of the region, much of the area has remained largely undisturbed. Foliage and grass coverage preserved the terraces and protected the archeological sites. This environment provided the U. S. Forest Service an opportunity to conduct surveys of the resources and offer interpretation programs for this unique group of resources. According to Lawrence Kingsbury, heritage program manager, the Payette National Forest used the multiple property nomination and interpretive materials to highlight the historic resources, as well as to gain a measure of protection for them. Kingsbury noted that "[t]he 19th-century gold rush resources were threatened.... In order to create a preservation awareness [sic], we invited university interests to investigate the Chinese sites. We created interpretive signage and historic monographs to educate the public. We provided tours.... After each archeological excavation, we produced reports (gray literature) for the interested archeological community."[5]

The Payette National Forest developed a self-guided interpretive tour for visitors, using a brochure and signs on the Old China Trail and at the gardens. The China Mountain Interpretive Site highlights the development of the gardens and their connection with the Chinese and the larger mining community. Signage highlights the Chinese settlers' use of terracing in garden design, an agricultural practice common in Guangdong province.[6] Additional interpretive signage at the Chinese Cemetery addresses burial practices. Site interpretation is provided in monographs and an artifact exhibit area available at the Warren Guard Station.[7] The Payette Heritage Program is working with the Wing Luke Asian Museum in Seattle, Washington, to increase the biographical information on the individuals who resided in the Warren area.

The discovery of gold was a major impetus to developing the American West. Towns literally materialized overnight to support the mining communities. The legacy of the Gold Rush is evident in Warren and other places in Idaho, Nevada, and California. Mining structures and material culture associated with mining contribute to the heritage of the western states. The interpretive program at Warren Mining District presents a view of this historic period through the prism of the Chinese experience.

Haraguchi Rice Mill
Hanalei, Hawaii

Located on the island of Kauai, Hanalei Valley was the major center of rice production in Hawaii. At its height, Hawaii was the third leading rice producer in the United States, behind Louisiana and South Carolina.[8] Rice was initially cultivated and produced by Chinese laborers, who started their own farms at the end of their contracts with the various agricultural plantations. Chinese workers made up the bulk of the plantation work force, but as their numbers declined because of the United States annexation of Hawaii and the Exclusion Act of 1882, Japanese laborers replaced them. Like their predecessors, Japanese laborers eventually left the plantations and bought farms, frequently from the exiting Chinese farmers.

Located within the Hanalei National Wildlife Reserve and administered by the United States Fish and Wildlife Service, the Haraguchi Rice Mill and farm were purchased by the Haraguchi family from a Chinese farmer named Man Sing in 1924. The diesel-powered mill was constructed in 1929, on the site of an older, water-powered wooden mill built by Chinese farmers in the 1880s.

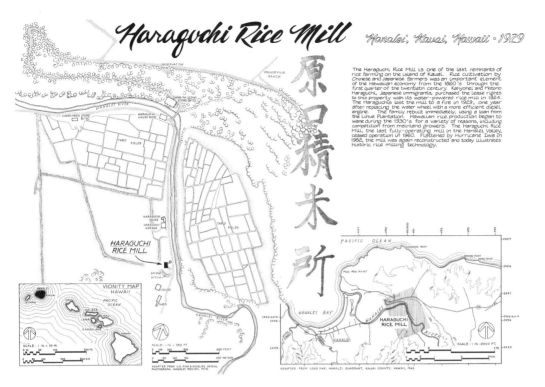

Haraguchi Rice Mill

Hanalei, Kauai, Hawaii • 1929

The Haraguchi Rice Mill is one of the last remnants of rice farming on the island of Kauai. Rice cultivation by Chinese and Japanese farmers was an important element of the Hawaiian economy from the 1880's through the first quarter of the twentieth century. Kahyohei and Motono Haraguchi, Japanese immigrants, purchased the lease rights to this property with its water-powered rice mill in 1924. The Haraguchis lost the mill to a fire in 1929, one year after replacing the water wheel with a more efficient diesel engine. The family rebuilt immediately, using a loan from the Lihue Plantation. Hawaiian rice production began to wane during the 1930's for a variety of reasons, including competition from mainland growers. The Haraguchi Rice Mill, the last fully-operating mill in the Hanalei Valley, ceased operation in 1960. Flattened by Hurricane Iwa in 1982, the mill was again reconstructed and today illustrates historic rice milling technology.

■ Rice holds a prominent place in the agricultural history of Hawaii. This drawing of the area surrounding the Haraguchi Rice Mill illustrates the setting for the mill within the agriculturally rich Hanalei Valley on Kauai in 1929.

Drawing by the Historic American Engineering Record

The milling area contains a strainer; two huskers; a polisher, which used cowhide belts; a grader that sorted the rice into three separate grades; and a bagging platform. Whereas the Japanese and Chinese practiced a similar method of rice cultivation, Japanese taste preferred a shorter grain of rice. In addition to the short grain staple rice, the Haraguchi Mill processed "mochi" rice, used in traditional sticky rice cakes made for the New Year's observance and other special occasions. The mill has been inoperative since 1961, and the remaining acreage of the Haraguchi farm has been converted to taro patches.

The history of rice and its cultivation in Hawaii is of increasing interest to visitors to the Hanalei National Wildlife Reserve. The mill (also known as the Ho'opulapula Haraguchi Rice Mill) offers tours for school groups and others and is developing a brochure about the site in collaboration with the Fish and Wildlife Service.[9] The mill provides a school curriculum package covering the agrarian, cultural, and economic contributions of the Chinese and Japanese immigrants. Additional interpretation is available at its website, http://www.haraguchiricemill.org. The Haraguchi Rice Mill is the only surviving rice mill in Hawaii, a remnant of an era of agricultural diversification on Kauai and a demographic shift in the Asian diaspora.

San Francisco Bay Maritime National Historic Park Shrimp Junk Project

San Francisco, California

Many Chinese immigrants arrived in the United States to work in the gold mines or railroad construction. Many also found work in the fishing industry. The Chinese were one of several ethnic minorities working the fishing trade in San Francisco Bay. For much of the second half of the 19th century, Chinese companies dominated the shrimping industry in San Francisco, catching and processing shrimp for Hawaiian and Asian markets. From the late 1850s to 1910, Chinese junks, single mast ships ranging from 30 to 50 feet in length and made almost entirely of redwood, were a common sight in the San Francisco Bay. In his *Tales of the Fish Patrol*, Jack London describes junk and shrimp trawling, offering insight into fishing industry in the San Francisco Bay during the early years of the 20th century.[10]

Chinese fishing villages, or camps, rimmed San Francisco Bay, and in coves at San Rafael, Richmond, as well as at Point San Pedro and around San Pablo Bay. The fishing villages are repositories of immigrant culture, and through archeological and historical surveys have provided information about these communities.

One of the largest of these fishing villages was the site of a shrimp junk reconstruction project by San Francisco Maritime National Historic Park, in conjunction with the China Camp State Park. Working from historical photographs, oral histories, and the archeological remains of two junks found in the mudflats at China Camp, the Junk Project crew, under the direction of John C. Muir of the San Francisco Maritime National Historic Park, replicated the design of these now extinct vessels.

■ Fishing junks, such as the one pictured pulling in nets ca. 1890s were a common sight in the San Francisco Bay. Chinese shrimp fishermen would cast upwards of 60 nets each day to fulfill the demand for shrimp in Hawaii and in Asian markets throughout the Pacific region.

Courtesy of San Francisco Maritime National Historic Park

■ The *Grace Quan* sails San Francisco Bay in one of its last sea trials prior to the official maiden voyage in April 2004. The ship helps the San Francisco Maritime National Historic Park staff interpret shrimp trawling and the lifeways of Chinese fishermen on the bay.

Courtesy of John C. Muir, San Francisco Maritime National Historic Park

Traditional Chinese boat construction methods and materials were used throughout the project. Muir traveled twice to modern-day traditional boatyards in southern China to learn the arts of firebending and edgenailing. In firebending, the planking wood is suspended over an open fire, with weights on the end. The wood is then carefully heated enough to let gravity create a bend. In edgenailing, the strength of the vessel is increased by nailing the planks to each other as well as to the interior structure. Triangular notches are carved along the bottom of a plank, and headless nails are driven down into the notch, essentially pinning the planks together. A special putty mixture, made from linseed or t'ung oil and crushed clam shells, is spread into the triangular notches to keep the nails from rusting.[11]

The 43-foot shrimp junk was built over the course of 6 months. The junk provides interpretation and research opportunities in illustrating the role of the Chinese as innovators in the fishing industry in northern California. The junk was constructed of redwood, with Douglas fir and white oak used in key structural areas. Hand-forged nails, pounded out on a coal forge, were used in edgenailing notches. Traditional oakum, or hemp-fiber caulking, was used to keep the boat watertight, and the rigging and sail were built using manila and cotton.

The completed junk was christened the *Grace Quan*, after the mother of the last remaining Chinese shrimp fisherman, Frank Quan, and launched on October 25, 2003. The junk was then towed to the Hyde Street Pier at the San Francisco Maritime National Historical Park, where she was outfitted for sail. The maiden voyage celebration occurred April 10, 2004, when the ship sailed along the San Francisco Bay waterfront.

The crews of the original shrimp junks were primarily from southern China's Pearl River Delta region.[12] Using large triangular nets staked into the mud flats, this technique took advantage of the incoming tide that brought shrimp into the nets, requiring the nets to be hauled in prior to ebb tide later that day. Shrimp junks set as many as 60 nets along the saltwater flats to the edge of deep fresh water and back. The day's catch was stored, sorted by size, and brought ashore, where the shrimp were boiled, then dried on wooden drying platforms on the hillside. The San Francisco Maritime staff plans to recreate the fishing techniques used by the crews as part of its interpretative program.

■ Despite their internment, some aspects of life continued as normal for Japanese Americans at Manzanar, with school-aged children and teens attending classes in 1943. The Teaching with Historic Places lesson plan encourages students to put themselves in the internees' place while learning about the events surrounding Japanese American internment.

Courtesy of Ansel Adams Manzanar War Relocation Camp Photograph Collection, Prints and Photographs Division, Library of Congress

Teaching with Historic Places, "The War Relocation Camps of World War II: When Fear Was Stronger than Justice"
National Register of Historic Places [http://www.cr.nps.gov/nr/twhp/wwwlps/lessons/89manzanar/89manzanar.htm]
The National Register of Historic Places has developed over 100 classroom-ready lesson plans through its Teaching with Historic Places program. These plans use National Register-listed properties to instruct readers on the significant themes, people, and events that shape American history and offer another way to experience historic places.

"The War Relocation Camps" lesson plan uses National Register and National Historic Landmark documentation to convey how the civil liberties of American citizens were violated by the forced removal and internment over 100,000 Japanese and Japanese Americans during World War II to relocation camps in Arkansas, Arizona, California, Colorado, Idaho, Utah, and Wyoming. The lesson plan's interpretation is supported by photographs, copies of flyers, and contemporary newspaper accounts.[13] "The War Relocation Camps" lesson plan recounts the story through the Manzanar Relocation Camp in California and Rowher Relocation Camp in Arkansas. Both sites retain a high degree of integrity, with Manzanar being the most highly restored relocation center and Rowher possessing the most original buildings and historic fabric.

"The War Relocation Camps" lesson plan discusses how Japanese families, forced to abandon their possessions and property, were crowded onto trains, and sent first to assembly centers, then to isolated relocation centers in seven states.[14] The lesson plan provides images of what the camps and their conditions were like and encourages students to relate to the internees.

■ *I Rei To*, or the soul-consoling tower, commemorates the 86 people interred at Manzanar. It is a site of reflection for visitors and is used for the inter-faith prayer service held during the annual pilgrimages.

Courtesy of Tom Walker

■ The Rohwer Veterans Memorial in Arkansas is a testament to the valor of the men of the 100th Battalion, 442nd Regimental Combat team. This all-Japanese American unit, filled with volunteers from relocation camps, was the most highly decorated unit of its size during World War II.

Courtesy of Kenneth Story

"The War Relocation Camps" lesson plan also highlights the patriotism of the *nisei*, or American-born children of Japanese immigrants, exemplified by the military accomplishments of the U.S. Army 442nd Regimental Combat Team and 100th Battalion, a segregated Japanese American volunteer unit that was highly decorated in World War II. Women volunteered for the Women's Army Corps and the Red Cross. Many of the volunteers came from the relocation camps. Using the memorial to their military exploits at the Rohwer Relocation Center Cemetery, the lesson plan addresses the contributions of Japanese Americans to the war effort.[15] *Nisei* patriotism clashed with resentment to internment, which led to altercations with military police and attempts by internees to regain their civil rights through lawsuits against the Federal Government. Despite these efforts, "The War Relocation Camps" notes that most internees never left the camps until the war's end.

Both of the camps featured in "The War Relocation Camps" lesson plan continue to convey the stories of their inhabitants long after their intended use. Former internees return to Manzanar and Rohwer to remember and to memorialize the internment period. An organized annual pilgrimage to Manzanar over the past 35 years prompted the inclusion of Manzanar National Historic Site in the National Park System, while Rohwer is a subject of study of internment in Arkansas for the Life Interrupted project, sponsored by the University of Arkansas Little Rock and the Japanese American National Museum.[16] "The War Relocation Camps" lesson plan offers an interpretation of the war homefront experience while providing the necessary historic context for understanding how an event such as the Japanese internment could take place and its impact not only on Japanese Americans, but all Americans.

United States Immigration Station, Angel Island
Tiburon Vicinity, California
Established in 1850 by President Millard Fillmore as a military reserve, the United States Immigration Station, Angel Island, is often known as the "Ellis Island" of the West Coast. From 1910 through 1940, approximately one million people were processed through the station. Most were of Asian descent—Chinese, Japanese, Korean, Filipinos, and Asian Indians—and included Australians, Russians, Mexicans, and Portuguese. During that period, approximately 250,000 Chinese and 150,000 Japanese immigrants were detained at Angel Island as a result of the laws prohibiting Chinese, and later, Japanese immigration to the

Hundreds of passengers, such as those pictured ca. 1920, disembarked regularly at the Angel Island Immigration Station during the early 20th century. Called the Guardian of the Western Gate, one million people entered the United States through the station, with the majority being of Asian descent.

Courtesy of the California Department of State Parks & Recreation

United States. Unlike the inviting image of the Statue of Liberty, the immigration station at Angel Island loomed as the "Guardian of the Western Gate."

Situated in San Francisco Bay, Angel Island's use as a de facto detention center reflects the government's attitude towards Asian immigration. Political and commercial interests in California viewed Chinese immigration as a threat to American society. State and federal legislators created laws such as the Exclusion Act of 1882 to stem the tide of Chinese arrivals. Constructed between 1905 and 1910, the immigration station held Chinese immigrants until their paperwork was approved, a process that could take weeks or even months. After passage of the National Origins Act of 1924, the Japanese were similarly detained. The immigration station was closed in 1940. During World War II, it was used as a prisoner-of-war camp.[17]

The immigration station and associated buildings were turned over to the California State Park System in 1963. While exploring the barracks scheduled for demolition, a ranger, Alexander Weiss, discovered the now-famous Chinese calligraphic poems carved into the barracks walls.[18] Efforts by the Angel Island Immigration Station Historic Committee (now the Angel Island Immigration Station Foundation), Weiss, and Paul Choy led to the conversion of the barracks into a museum, with exhibits that relate to the immigrants' experience.

Much of the focus of the museum's interpretation is on the attitudes, hopes, and fears of the immigrants played out against the larger context of the governmental immigration policy. Additional interpretation is offered through a traveling exhibit sponsored by the Angel Island Immigration Station Foundation, *Gateway to Gold Mountain: The Angel Island Experience* and the foundation's website, http://www.asiif.org. The foundation conducted oral histories of former detainees that formed the basis for the book, *Island: Poetry and History of Immigrants on Angel Island.*[19]

Conclusion

Asian heritage has shaped the development of the United States and is increasingly interpreted at historic sites throughout the nation—from the Manzanar Relocation Camp to the banks of the Merrimack River during the dragon boat races in Lowell. Asian influence extends beyond the Chinatowns and Japantowns to places associated with other national historical themes, such as mining, maritime trade, and agricultural technology.

More than ever, historic preservation must convey American stories—great and small—associated with the growth of a nation. The multiplicity of views and opinions that emerge require new approaches through which to examine the nation's cultural heritage.

■ Delays in processing new arrivals at the Angel Island Immigration Station could take anywhere from days to months. Some Chinese detainees carved poems into the barracks walls to express their sadness while waiting to leave. These poems have become part of the historic record of the immigration station.

Courtesy of Surrey Blackburn

ENDNOTES

1. To avoid creating ethnic enclaves, the Indochina Migration and Refugee Assistance Act of 1975 sought to disperse the Cambodian and Vietnamese refugees throughout the country. The Boston area became a primary area of resettlement. The Refugee Act of 1980 provided funds to towns such as Lowell to accommodate the influx of Cambodians, Vietnamese, and Laotians. See Franklin Odo, ed., *The Columbia Documentary History of the Asian American Experience* (New York: Columbia University Press, 2002), 407-408.

2. Martha Norkunas discusses the Cambodian community's presence in the ethnically diverse and monument-filled city of Lowell in *Monuments and Memories: History and Representation in Lowell, Massachusetts* (Washington, DC: Smithsonian Institution Press, 2002), 34-35, 59-60, 167.

3. In Cambodia, the Water Festival, or *Bon Om Puk*, takes place on the Mekong River during the full moon of the eleventh month at the end of the rainy season. National Park Service employees helped construct long boats for the 2001 Southeast Asian Water Festival. See "Singing Hope Along the Mekong River," in *Tzu Chi Quarterly* 8, no. 1(Spring 2001); "Cambodian Odyssey: Executive Summary, Lowell Delegation to Cambodia June 24-July 2, 2001" (Lowell, MA: Lowell National Historic Park, 2001).

4. Federal Writers' Projects of the Works Progress Administration, American Guide Series, *Idaho: A Guide in Words and Pictures,* 3rd Printing (New York and Oxford, UK: Oxford Press, 1968), 122. While the names China Mountain and China Trail are toponyms, place-names that serve a specific function, it is safe to assume that the names were not given by the Chinese immigrants.

5. Concerns over looting, flea market treasure seekers, authorized gold mining, and rock harvesting for resurfacing roads fueled the need for preservation of the resources. Lawrence Kingsbury, electronic correspondence with the author, December 18, 2003.

6. Guangdong province is the place from which the majority of immigrants hailed. Earlier settlers to Warren claimed much of the better farmland, but Chinese familiar with terracing techniques were able to take advantage of the fertile land of the available steep mountainsides. The terraces are cut into the slope, and planted with crops and other plant life. The technique requires a close proximity to water, which China Mountain has in abundance from China Creek and the Salmon River.

7. Exhumation was an important burial practice for overseas Chinese. When a male immigrant died, his body would be prepared and sent back home to China by his family. *Huiguan*, associations of people from the same districts, would have paid for deceased members without family to cover the expense. They provided a support system for migratory laborers with strong ties to districts, occupations, and dialects. Twenty-nine of the 35 individuals interred in the cemetery were returned home. For the authoritative text on the associations, see Him Mark Lai, "Historical Development of the Chinese Consolidated Benevolent Association/ Huiguan System," in *Chinese America: History and Perspectives, Journal of the Chinese Historical Society of America* 1(1987): 13-52. For discussions on the practice of exhumation, see National Register of Historic Places, *Chinese Cemetery, Idaho County, Idaho. National Register #9400270*; Sucheng Chan, *Twayne's Immigrant History of America Series, Asian Americans: An Interpretative History* (New York: Twayne Publishers, 1991), 64-65; and Payette National Forest, Heritage Program, "The Chinese Cemetery at Warren," (U.S. Department of Agriculture, U.S. Forest Service, July 2002, monograph).

The monographs offer the interested visitor more in-depth information on individuals and practices of the Chinese in and around Warren. See Sheila D. Reddy, "Mountain Garden, Mountain Stew" (McCall, ID: U.S. Department of Agriculture, U.S. Forest Service, February 1994); Lawrence A. Kingsbury, "Celadon Slope

Garden, *Circa* 1870-1902: A Chinese Sojourner Occupation on the Payette National Forest" (U.S. Department of Agriculture, Forest Service, December 1990); Lawrence A. Kingsbury, "Chinese Properties Listed in the National Register," in *CRM* 17, no. 2 (1994): 23-24; National Register of Historic Places, *Chinese Sites in the Warren Mining District Multiple Property Survey, Idaho County, Idaho. National Register #1696100*.

8. Rice cultivation in North America dates back to the late 1600s, coming through western Africa, but the Chinese and Japanese have a rice tradition dating back 4,000 to 8,000 years. The types of grains (*Oryza sativa*) and techniques (transplanting rice seedlings after 30-50 days into paddies) used in Hawaii equate with Asian rice traditions. See *Rice Almanac: Source Book for the Most Important Economic Activity on Earth*. Third Edition (Oxon, UK: CABI Publishing, 2002), 1-4; and John Wesley Coulter and Chee Kwon Chen, "Chinese Rice Farmers in Hawaii," *University of Hawaii Bulletin* 16, no. 5(1937): 18.

9. Currently, the mill is closed to the public while undergoing restoration. However Ho'opulapula Haraguchi Rice Mill is working with the U.S. Fish and Wildlife Service to develop a guided tour to meet the requests for visitation.

10. London's description of his time as an officer for the California Fish Commission also provides examples of negative stereotypes accorded ethnic minorities, Asians in particular. See Jack London, *Tales of the Fish Patrol* (Cleveland, OH and New York: International Fiction Library, 1905).

11. John Muir provided the descriptions of the various construction techniques used to build the *Grace Quan*. John C. Muir, electronic correspondence with the author, January 5, 2004.

12. For a fuller description of the shrimp harvesting technique, see "All in a Day's Work: San Francisco Shrimp Junks," by John C. Muir at Native Sons of the Golden West website, http://www.nsgw.org/projects/shrimpboat/dayswork.html; accessed December 8, 2003.

13. Some of the most famous photographs of Manzanar came from a photographic essay by Ansel Adams of the Manzanar relocation camp and offer visual documentation of the isolated locations and harsh conditions provided for these incarcerated citizens. His interest stemmed from his relationship with Harry Oye, a long-time *issei* employee of Adams. Adams commented in his 1965 letter to the Library of Congress donating the collection, "The purpose of my work was to show how these people, suffering under a great injustice, and loss of property, businesses and professions, had overcome the sense of defeat and dispair [sic] by building for themselves a vital community in an arid (but magnificent) environment... All in all, I think this Manzanar Collection is an important historical document, and I trust it can be put to good use." The collection is available in print, *Born Free and Equal: The Story of Loyal Japanese Americans* (Bishop, CA: Spotted Dog Press, 2001) and through the Library of Congress, Prints and Photographs Collection in Washington, DC and online at "Prints and Photographs Online Catalog-Ansel Adams' Photographs of Japanese American Internment," at http://lcweb2.loc.gov/pp/manzhtml/manzabt.html; maintained by the Library of Congress, accessed April 10, 2004.

14. For example, at Manzanar, 10,000 people lived in pine framed, tar-paper covered barracks, with communal messes (cafeterias) and bathrooms. The internees were expected to help support their internment—with industrial and agricultural complexes. See National Register of Historic Places, *Manzanar Relocation Center, Inyo County, California. National Register #76000484*; Jeffery F. Burton, Mary M. Farrell, Florence B. Lord, and Richard W. Lord, *Confinement and Ethnicity: An Overview of World War II Japanese American Relocation Sites*, Publications in Anthropology 74 (Tucson, AZ: Western Archeological and Conservation Center, U.S. Department of the Interior, National Park Service, 1999).

15. See National Historic Landmarks Survey, *Rohwer Relocation Center Cemetery, Desha County, Arkansas;* and Burton, et al., *Confinement and Ethnicity*, 254-257.

16. The Manzanar Committee sponsors trips for surviving detainess each year, one of several pilgrimages made to the site. Other relocation centers host similar pilgrimages. Rohwer hosted a homecoming in September 2004 as a part of the "Life Interrupted: The Japanese American Experience in WWII Arkansas" project, which features exhibits at three locations near Little Rock and a conference to accompany the homecoming. See "The Manzanar Committee Online" at http://www.manzanarcommittee.org; maintained by the Japanese American Network, accessed April 14, 2004; and "Life Interrupted: The Japanese American Experience in WWII Arkansas" at http://www.lifeinterrupted.org/; maintained by the University of Arkansas Little Rock, accessed April 14, 2004.

17. See National Register of Historic Places, *Angel Island, Marin County, California. National Register #71000164*; National Historic Landmark Survey, *U.S. Immigration Station Angel Island, Tiburon, California*; See Atim Oton's review of "Gateway to Golden Mountain: the Angel Island Experience, part of the exhibit *Tin See Do: the Angel Island Experience*, at the Ellis Island Immigration Museum, Ellis Island, New York; March 8-May 31, 2003," in *CRM: The Journal of Heritage Stewardship* 1, no. 1(Fall 2003): 135-137.

18. The isolation of being neither home nor able to leave the immigration center produced profound sorrow for many detainees. Time at Angel Island was spent being examined at the hospital, being interrogated, and being housed in barracks. Some carved poetry into the barracks walls that reflect the hardship and indignity. See National Historic Landmarks Survey, *Angel Island*; and "The Angel Island Immigration Foundation" at http://www.asiif. org; accessed February 6, 2004.

19. Him Mark Lai, Genny Lim, and Judy Yung, *Island: Poetry and History of Chinese Immigrants on Angel Island, 1910-1940* (Seattle: University of Washington Press, 1991).

APPENDIX

Asian Heritage in the National Park Service Cultural Resources Programs

This list represents a compilation of the properties associated with Asian heritage documented in the National Park Service's cultural resources programs (National Register of Historic Places, National Historic Landmarks, and Historic American Buildings Survey/Historic American Engineering Record/Historic American Landscapes Survey). It is not exhaustive, but illustrates examples of Asian properties that have already been documented and/or recognized. Further investigation of the files may yield additional entries.

National Register of Historic Places
The following National Register properties are associated with Asian heritage. Each entry is listed by state, followed by a brief statement of what makes it significant to Asian heritage.

Alaska
Stedman-Thomas Historic District (Ketchikan, Ketchikan Gateway County) is a community of multiple Asian groups that was developed during the fishing industry in the region from the 1900s to the 1940s. Chinese, Filipino, Korean, and Japanese families opened many of the earliest businesses and established this commercial center in the city.

American Samoa
Faga Village Site (T'au, Manu'a County) is an archeological site associated with the title of Tui Manu'a (the highest title in Samoan culture) and as the oldest Samoan village. Faga Village is still used for agricultural and funerary purposes.

California
Castroville Japanese Language School (Castroville, Monterey County) illustrates Japanese American cultural and educational development in the early 20th century. It served as a language school, meeting hall, and Buddhist temple.

Oroville Chinese Temple (Oroville, Butte County) served as a community center for many early Chinese immigrants who arrived during the Gold Rush era. In 1959, the Temple Complex became a public museum dedicated to Chinese culture and tradition.

Point Reyes National Seashore (Point Reyes, Marin County) was where the Spanish ship, the *San Agustin*, shipwrecked in 1595 with Filipino sailors aboard. The surviving crew eventually traveled by land to Mexico.

Federated States of Micronesia
Leluh Ruins (Leluh, Kosrae County) are associated with the rise of the Kosraen society, an early Pacific culture. The archeological site may yield information on Kosraen, Micronesian, and Pacific societies.

Rull Men's Meeting House (Rull Municipality, Yap District) was where men gathered to plan war strategy, perform rites of passage for young men, and address other important aspects of social life. This meetinghouse, or *faluw*, is significant to the ethnic heritage of Micronesians and may yield information about this culture's early history.

Guam

Fafai Beach Site (Tumon Bay, Guam County) contains the ruins of six-to-eight housing structures of the Chamorro people. Fafai Beach Site is significant for its potential for archeological research on cultural change and settlement patterns of people of Guam.

Gadao's Cave (Inarajan Bay, Guam County) is an archeological site containing pictographs and petroglyphs and is likely to yield important information about the early history of Guam.

Umatac Outdoor Library (Umatac, Guam County) is the first public library built in Southern Guam under the direction of Francisco Quinta Sanchez (1898-1954), an early 20th-century pioneer of education and a politician from Umatac. The Umatac Outdoor Library is significant to Chamorro people and reflects their resolve to improve their lives.

Hawaii

Chee Ying Society (Honokaa, Hawaii County) or "Chinese Clubhouse," was a community center for members of the Hung Men Society, a secret society created in China in 1631. It is one of the few remaining society clubhouses in Hawaii.

Chinatown Historic District (Honolulu, Honolulu County) was a commercial and residential center for Chinese immigrants and other Asian groups. In its buildings, institutions, and people, the Chinatown Historic District reflects the city's role as a center for many diverse cultures.

Chinese Tong Houses of Maui Island (Lahaina, Maui County) were constructed for members of the Chinese Hoong Moon secret societies in the first decade of the 20th century. Tongs provided aid to individuals from the same district or province. Only three of the original six houses remain.

The Chee Kung Tong Society Building is the home to the mother society of tongs in the United States. The building may provide information about an important aspect of the Chinese immigrant experience in Hawaii at the turn of the 20th century.

The Ket Hing Society Building is one of three remaining houses associated with the Hoong Moon Tong in Maui. The building represents Chinese immigration heritage in Hawaii.

The Wo Hing Society Building is affiliated with the Chee Kung Tong that provided aid to Chinese immigrants in Hawaii. The building is considered to be the finest of the remaining tong buildings and houses a museum about tongs and the lives of overseas Chinese at the turn of the 20th century.

Daifukuji Soto Zen Mission (Kona, Hawaii County) is significant as an example of Buddhist temple architecture constructed in the early 20th century in Hawaii. The building blends construction techniques from Hawaii's plantation tradition with Japanese temple design.

Haraguchi Rice Mill (Hanalei, Kauai County) is the last remaining rice mill in Hawaii and reflects the combined cultural imprint of the Chinese and Japanese in Hawaii.

Hawaii Shingon Mission (Honolulu, Honolulu County) is the mother church for the Shingon sect in Hawaii and one of the few remaining Japanese Buddhist missions of its type in Hawaii.

Kawailoa Temple (Haleiwa, Honolulu County) is one of the few remaining structures that incorporates indoor/outdoor concepts of Japanese architecture by the use of moveable *shoji* doors. The Kawailoa Temple served as the cultural and social focal point for Japanese plantation workers because it incorporated a language school and clubs, and hosted community celebrations.

Kyoto Gardens of Honolulu Memorial Park (Honolulu, Honolulu County) contains the finest examples of Japanese traditional-style structures and gardens built outside of Japan.

Lihue Hongwanji Mission (Lihue, Kauai County) is the oldest Japanese Buddhist mission still extant on Kauai. Also serving as a language school, the mission helped maintain the heritage of 20th-century Japanese immigrants.

Seto Building (Kapaa, Kauai County) combines the Chinese aesthetic and commercial building forms and symbolizes the commercial and cultural development of the Hawaiian Islands.

Toyo Theatre (Honolulu, Honolulu County) is a Japanese language movie theater. An example of Edo period architectural design, it was modeled after the famous Ieyasu Shrine in Nikko, Japan.

Wakamiya Inari Shrine (Oahu, Honolulu County) is dedicated to the Inari Shinto sect that is associated with the working class Japanese, including agricultural laborers, in Hawaii in the early 20th century. It is the only example of Inari traditional shrine architecture in the region.

Idaho

The Chinese Sites in the Warren Mining District Multiple Property Survey (Warren vicinity, Idaho County) provides an example of identifying and interpreting a range of resources to tell the story of Chinese heritage in the United States. The following interrelated sites located in Payette National Forest tell the story of the Chinese miners in the West.

Ah Toy Garden (Warren vicinity, Idaho County) is a terraced garden created by the Chinese community to grow vegetables and fruits so that traditional diets could be maintained while community members worked the mines around the Warren Mining District. One of three such gardens in the area, Ah Toy Garden also produced vegetables, strawberries, grapes, and rhubarb for commercial sale.

Celadon Slope Garden (Warren vicinity, Idaho County) is the second of three terraced gardens on China Mountain in the Warren Mining District. It was used by the Chinese community until 1902.

Chi-Sandra Garden (Warren vicinity, Idaho County) Chi-Sandra is the third terraced garden in the Warren Mining District associated with the Chinese miners who lived and worked there.

China Trail (Warren vicinity, Idaho County) is a pack trail that connects the three terraced gardens on China Mountain. Chinese farmers used the trail to move produce from the gardens to the mining camps and local markets.

Chinese Cemetery (Warren vicinity, Idaho County) holds the remains of Chinese miners who worked placer claims in the Warren Mining District. Although many of the bodies have been exhumed and returned to China, the Chinese Cemetery may hold information about funerary practices of Chinese immigrants in Idaho.

Chinese Mining Camp Archeological Site (Warren vicinity, Idaho County) may hold information about daily life among the Chinese miners. The site contains a the remains of a blacksmith forge, a building with a kitchen and dining area, a small garden, and remnants of placer mines.

Polly Bemis House (Warren, Idaho County) belonged to a local Chinese woman who lived in the area from 1894 to 1933. Built during 1923 and 1924, her home is an example of a whipsawn lumber log cabin. The property provides insight into the struggles immigrant women faced in the rural Northwest in the early 20th century.

Moore Gulch Chinese Mining Site (Pierce, Clearwater County) may yield important information about the mining techniques of Chinese immigrants. The site contains living quarters, mine tailings, ditches, and other features associated with a mining community in the second half of the 19th century.

Massachusetts
Lowell National Historic Park (Lowell, Middlesex County) is known for its connections to the rise of the industrial age in the United States. It is also a significant site for the more recent Cambodian community, which is the largest Asian group in the city. Cambodian residents and organizations cooperate with the park on festivals and the park has provided a place for cultural organizations to meet and perform.

Minnesota
Jun Fujita Cabin (International Falls, St. Louis County) contains architectural elements consistent with Japanese country house design. The cabin was a retreat and a source of inspiration for the owner's artistic work.

Utah
Golden Spike National Historic Site (Promontory Summit, Box Elder County) commemorates the completion of the first transcontinental railroad and the role of Chinese immigrants in its construction. The Central Pacific Railroad Company employed an estimated 10,000 to 12,000 Chinese laborers who built the western portion of the transcontinental railroad system.

Washington
Bainbridge Island Filipino Community Hall (Bainbridge Island, Kitsap County) is the first Filipino community hall in Washington State. Its construction by the Bainbridge Island Filipino Farmers' Association in 1943 coincided with a rise in the Filipino population, who were important contributors to the region's agricultural production.

Chinese Baptist Church (Seattle, King County) is linked to the growth of the Chinese community in Seattle in the early 20th century. The church provided services for the community and is a repository of information about Chinese immigrants in Seattle.

Mukai Cold Process Plant (Vashon Island, King County) represents the role of Japanese immigrants in the development of the agricultural industry in early 20th-century Washington State. It was a successful plant, using new technologies to preserve and transport berries to market.

Nihon Go Gakko (Tacoma, Pierce County) also known as the Tacoma Japanese Language School, was constructed in 1922 and is one of the few remaining buildings associated with the Japanese community in Tacoma. It served as a center for the Japanese American community prior to the outbreak of World War II.

Nihon Go Gakko (Seattle, King County) was the oldest functioning Japanese language school in the continental United States. Established in 1902, the language school served the Japanese community until 1942, when it was confiscated by the U.S. government and turned into an Army training center. Twenty-seven Japanese Americans families lived temporarily in the building's classrooms after their return from World War II internment.

Nippon Kan Hall (Seattle, King County) was a social and cultural center for Japanese Americans and served as a hotel for Japanese visitors and immigrants and as a theater.

Seattle Chinatown Historic District (Seattle, King County), also known as the International District, was home to the most extensive Asian community in Washington state. It contains examples of Asian design aesthetics combined with Western architecture, which give the district its distinctive character.

National Historic Landmarks
The following National Historic Landmark properties are associated with Asian heritage. Each entry is listed by state and includes a brief statement of what makes it significant to Asian heritage.

Arkansas
Rohwer Relocation Center and Memorial Cemetery (Rohwer, Desha County) is one of two World War II relocation camps in the state. The camp held 8,475 people of Japanese ancestry and was occupied for 43 months. The site contains two monuments and one of three surviving relocation cemeteries.

California
Gakuen Hall (Walnut Grove, Sacramento County) is a surviving example of a Japanese culture and language school designed and built by the Japanese in response to the 1921 California public school segregation laws. Today it serves as a community center for the Japanese American community, including residents who originally planned and created Gakuen Hall.

Harada House (Riverside, Riverside County) was home to the Harada family, who tested the constitutionality of anti-alien land laws in the United States. In *California v. Harada* (1916-1918), the state upheld the right of native-born citizens of the United States to own land, regardless of ethnicity.

Isleton Chinese and Japanese Commercial Districts (Isleton, Sacramento County) was a busy multi-ethnic commercial district from the late 1890s until the 1940s. The district represents a secondary stage of migration for Asian immigrants in California.

Little Tokyo Historic District (Los Angeles, Los Angeles County) was the largest Japanese community in the United States prior to World War II. Vestiges of Japanese ethnic heritage still exist at its commercial core, including buildings and signage associated with Japanese American businesses.

Locke Historic District (Locke, Sacramento County) is the most important example of a rural Chinese American community in the United States. Today's inhabitants are the descendants of Chinese laborers who developed the Sacramento-San Joaquin River Delta. (Also documented by Historic American Buildings Survey.)

Manzanar War Relocation Center (Independence vicinity, Inyo County) was the first Japanese American internment camp created during World War II. The camp housed over 10,000 persons of Japanese descent, the vast majority of whom were American citizens. (Also documented by Historic American Buildings Survey.)

Presidio of San Francisco (San Francisco, Marin County) includes two buildings significant to Japanese American history. Building 35 was the site where Executive Order 9066 was issued. It served as the headquarters for the Western Defense Command (WDC), the U.S. Army command responsible for implementation and enforcement of the order. Building 640 contained the classrooms for the Military Intelligence Service Language School (MISLS) where MIS and Japanese civilians taught the Japanese language to military personnel and translated captured documents.

Walnut Grove Chinese American Historic District (Walnut Grove, Sacramento County) was constructed as a commercial district for Chinese agricultural workers in the Sacramento-San Joaquin River Delta region.

Walnut Grove Japanese American Historic District (Walnut Grove, Sacramento County) was built and designed by Japanese Americans and is associated with the community's agricultural labor in the Sacramento-San Joaquin River Delta region.

District of Columbia
United States Supreme Court Building (Washington, DC) is significant for its association with four cases defending the civil rights of Japanese Americans during World War II: *Hirabayashi v. United States* (1943), *Yasui v. United States* (1943), *Korematsu v. United States* (1944), and *Endo v. United States* (1944). Only one of the four cases resulted in a successful verdict for its plaintiff.

Federated States of Micronesia
Nan Madol (Madolenihmw, Pohnpei County) is a 321-acre complex of man-made basalt islands and architectural remains built atop an atoll. This site may yield information about Pohnpeian early history.

Hawaii
Hokukano-Ualapue Complex (Ualapue vicinity, Maui County) contains six temple platforms and two fishponds constructed between A.D. 1500 and contact with the West in 1778.

Huilua Fishpond (Oahu, Honolulu County) is one of the few surviving fishponds out of an estimated 97 ponds that once existed along the coast of Oahu. These fishponds represent an important Hawaiian form of aquaculture—fish farms that hatched and raised fish for local consumption.

Iolani Palace (Honolulu, Honolulu County) was the official residence of the last two rulers of Hawaii, King Kalakaua and Queen Lili'uokalani, before the transfer of sovereignty to the United States in 1898. It is the only official royal palace in the United States.

Kalaupapa Leprosy Settlement (Kalaupapa, Kalawao County) was the site of a leper colony, established in 1866, to curb an epidemic among native Hawaiians. (Also documented by Historic American Buildings Survey.)

Kamakahonu (Kailua-Kona, Hawaii County) was the home of King Kamehameha I, who unified the Hawaiian Islands, from 1812 until his death in 1819. This was also the site where the first missionaries landed in Hawaii in 1818.

Keauhou Holua Slide (Kailua-Kona, Hawaii County) is one of the best-preserved and largest *holuas*, or sled runs, in Hawaii.

Mookini Heiau (Kohala, Hawaii County) is an important religious site for Polynesians in Hawaii. It is associated with and located near the birthplace of King Kamehameha I, the founder of the Kingdom of Hawaii.

Puukohola Heiau (Kawaihae, Hawaii County) is the site where Kamehameha ascended to the kingship of the Hawaiian Islands in 1791. The event took place in a temple built by Kamehameha to honor the war god, Kukailimoku.

Wailua Complex of Heiaus (Wailua, Kauai County) contains important archeological remains associated with Hawaiian cultural history. The complex includes a petroglyph site, four *heiaus* or shrines, and a bell stone.

Minnesota

Fort Snelling (Minneapolis, Hennepin County) was the location for the Military Intelligence Service Language School (MISLS). Second-generation Japanese Americans, or *nisei*, as well as enlisted European American soldiers, served as linguists during the war and trained with the MISLS. During 1944-1945, the school housed 3,000 students and 160 instructors in more than 125 classrooms.

Missouri

Missouri Botanical Garden (St. Louis, St. Louis County) houses a Japanese Tea House and the largest authentic Japanese garden in North America. For the past 27 years, during each Labor Day weekend, the site hosts the Japanese Festival that celebrates Japanese people and culture. (Also documented by Historic American Buildings Survey.)

Oklahoma

Fort Sill (Fort Sill, Comanche County) is associated with Japanese Americans through its use as an internment camp. From March 1942 until Spring 1943, it held 700 "enemy aliens."

Texas

Fort Sam Houston (San Antonio, Bexar County) held 40 Japanese Hawaiians and 300 Alaskan Eskimos in the camp for nine days before they were transferred to Camp Lordsburg in New Mexico County during World War II.

Historic American Buildings Survey
The following Historic American Buildings Survey properties are associated with Asian heritage. Each entry is listed by state and includes a brief statement of what makes it significant to Asian heritage.

California

Auburn-Chinese Section (Auburn, Placer County) was home to Chinese laborers working on the transcontinental railroad in the 1850s and contains buildings associated with the Chinese community.

Chinese Joss House (Weaverville, Trinity County) is the oldest continuously used Chinese temple in California. Built in 1874, the "Temple of the Forest beneath the Clouds" exhibits traditional Taoist architectural detailing and contains artifacts associated with the Chinese community in 19th-century California.

Vedanta Society (San Francisco, San Francisco County) also known as the Hindu Society, was the headquarters and a place of worship for followers of Vedantism, a branch of Hinduism. Built between 1905 and 1906, the building reflects an Asian Indian temple design aesthetic.

District of Columbia
Chinese Community Church (Washington, DC) was constructed in 1956 for the Chinatown community and made use of Chinese design motifs. Today, the church serves as a Chinese community center.

Idaho
Chinese Roasting Pit (Salmon vicinity, Lemhi County) was used by Chinese miners who wintered in and around Salmon during the Gold Rush era in Idaho.

New York
Kykuit, Japanese Gardens and Teahouse (Pocantico Hills, New York) follows the style of a *ryoan-ji* temple garden, typical of western Kyoto. Japanese carpenters and gardeners Takahashi and Uyeda designed the gardens and the original teahouse, which was redesigned by architect Junzo Yoshimura, after the Katsura Imperial Villa in Kyoto.

Washington
Kosai Farm (Auburn, King County) is important in the political history of Japanese Americans because it served as the basis for a legal case that challenged the state's Anti-Alien Land Law.

Historic American Engineering Record
The following Historic American Engineering Record properties are associated with Asian heritage. Each entry is listed by state and includes a brief statement of what makes it significant to Asian heritage.

Hawaii
Hanalei Pier (Hanalei, Kauai County) is one of the last vestiges of rice production in Hawaii and is significant for its role in agricultural and transportation history. Chinese and Japanese rice producers used the pier to transport their crop to markets on other islands and on the United States mainland.

Washington
Chinese Workers House (Port Gamble, Kitsap County) provided segregated housing accommodations for Chinese workers of the logging industries at Port Gamble, who were part of a larger workforce that included Hawaiians. Many of the Chinese served as cooks for the other laborers.

Selected Bibliography

Burton, Jeffery F., Mary M. Farrell, Florence B. Lord, and Richard W. Lord. *Confinement and Ethnicity: An Overview of World War II Japanese American Relocation Sites, Publications in Anthropology* 74. Tucson, AZ: U.S. Department of the Interior, National Park Service, Western Archeological and Conservation Center, 1999.

Chan, Sucheng. *Asian Americans: An Interpretive History.* Twayne's Immigrant History of America Series, New York: Twayne Publishing, 1991.

—. *This Bittersweet Soil: The Chinese in California Agriculture, 1860-1910.* Los Angeles and Berkeley: University of California Press, 1991.

Chinese Historical Society of America. *Chinese America: History and Perspectives.* The Journal of the Chinese Historical Society of America. Multiple volumes.

Cohen, Lucy M. *Chinese in the Post-Civil War South: A People Without a History.* Baton Rouge: Louisiana State University Press, 1984.

Coolidge, Mary Roberts. *Chinese Immigration.* New York: Holt and Company, 1909.

Conroy, Hilary. *The Japanese Frontier in Hawaii, 1868-1898.* Los Angeles and Berkeley: University of California Press, 1953.

Daniels, Roger. *Asian America: Chinese and Japanese in the United States Since 1850.* Seattle: University of Washington Press, 1988.

Dubrow, Gail, with Donna Graves. *Sento at Sixth and Main: Preserving Landmarks of Japanese American Heritage.* Seattle: Seattle Arts Commission [University of Washington Press], 2002.

Espina, Marina. *Filipinos in Louisiana.* New Orleans, LA: A.F. Laborde and Sons, 1988.

Espiritu, Yen Le. *Filipino American Lives.* Philadelphia: Temple University Press, 1995.

—. *Asian American Panethnicity: Bridging Institutions and Identities.* Philadelphia: Temple University Press, 1992.

Kim, Hyung-chan. *Asian American Studies: An Annotated Bibliography and Research Guide.* Westport, CT: Greenwood Publishing, 1989.

—. *Dictionary of Asian American History.* Westport, CT: Greenwood Publishing, 1986.

Kitano, Harry. *Japanese Americans: The Evolution of a Subculture.* Englewood Cliffs, NJ: Prentice-Hall, 1976.

Kitano, Harry H. L. and Roger Daniels. *Asian Americans: Emerging Minorities.* Englewood Cliffs, NJ: Prentice-Hall, 1988.

Lancaster, Clay. *The Japanese Influence in America.* New York: W. H. Rawls [Twayne Publishers], 1963.

Lai, Him Mark. *Becoming Chinese American: A History of Communities and Institutions.* Walnut Creek, CA: Alta Mira, 2004.

—. *From Overseas Chinese to Chinese America: A History of the Development of Chinese Society During the Twentieth Century*. Hong Kong: Joint Publishing Company, 1992.

—. *A History Reclaimed: An Annotated Bibliography of Chinese Language Materials on the Chinese in America*. Los Angeles: Asian American Studies Center, University of California Los Angeles, 1986.

—. "Chinese." In Stephan Thernstrom, editor, *Harvard Encyclopedia of American Ethnic Groups*. Cambridge, MA: Belknap Press, 1980, 217-234.

Lazzerini, Edward J. *The Asian Peoples of Southern Louisiana: An Ethnohistory*. New Orleans: University of New Orleans, Center for the Pacific Rim, 1990.

Lee, Joann Faung Jean. *Asian American Experiences in the United States: Oral Histories of First to Fourth Generation Americans From China, the Philippines, Japan, India, the Pacific Islands, Vietnam, and Cambodia*. Jefferson, NC: McFarland and Company, 1991.

Lee, Rose Hum. *The Chinese in the United States of America*. Hong Kong: Hong Kong University Press, 1960.

Lowe, Lisa. *Immigrant Acts: On Asian American Cultural Politics*. Durham, NC: Duke University Press, 1996.

Mangiafico, Luciano. *Contemporary American Immigrants: Patterns of Filipino, Korean, and Chinese Settlement in the United States*. New York: Praeger Publishing, 1998.

Odo, Franklin, editor. *The Columbia Documentary History of the Asian American Experience*. New York: Columbia University Press, 2002.

Okihiro, Gary Y. *The Columbia Guide to Asian American History*. New York: Columbia University Press, 2001.

Okihiro, Gary Y., editor. *Privileging Positions: The Sites of Asian American Studies*. Pullman: Washington State University Press, 1995.

Okihiro, Gary Y., Shirley Hune, Arthur A. Hansen, and John M. Liu, editors. *Reflections on Shattered Windows: Promise and Prospects for Asian American Studies*. Pullman: Washington State University Press, 1988.

Takaki, Ronald. *Strangers From a Different Shore: A History of Asian Americans*. Boston: Little, Brown, 1989.

Tchen, John Kuo Wei. *New York Before Chinatown: Orientalism and the Shaping of American Culture, 1776-1882*. Baltimore: Johns Hopkins University Press, 1999.

Upton, Dell, editor. *America's Architectural Roots: Ethnic Groups That Built America*. New York: Preservation Press, 1986.

Wegars, Priscilla, editor. *Hidden Heritage: Historical Archaeology of the Overseas Chinese*. Amityville, NY: Baywood Publishing Company, 1993.

List of Federal Legislation related to Asian Groups in the United States

Since 1790, federal legislation has been enacted to prevent people of Asian descent from being fully active participants in American society. This listing of federal legislation against Asian and other nonwhite persons does not include the numerous state and local laws designed to discriminate against Asian groups in those jurisdictions.

Naturalization Act, 1790: The law established two years of residence and that the individual must be a "free white person" as requirements for citizenship.

An Act to Prohibit the "Coolie Trade" by American Citizens in American Vessels, 1862: The act intended to curtail the "coolie" trade, indentured Chinese labor used by the British, as a source of cheap labor. It coincides with the Civil War and the issue of slave labor in the United States.

Fourteenth Amendment to the U.S. Constitution, 1868: Intended to protect the rights of African Americans against legislation from individual states, Section 1 of the Fourteenth Amendment was invoked to overturn many West Coast discriminatory laws targeted at Asian Americans. It protected the rights of "any persons" to due process and equal protection, clarifying the boundaries of constitutional safeguards for everyone in the United States.

Burlingame-Seward Treaty, 1868: The treaty allowed for free migration and emigration between China and the United States but upheld the decision not to allow naturalization of Chinese as United States citizens, and vice versa.

An Act Supplementary to the Acts in Relation to Immigration, a.k.a. the Page Law, 1875: Purported to deter the importation of women for prostitution, it effectively deterred female Asian immigrants and hindered the development of Asian communities in the United States for decades.

An Act to Execute Certain Treaty Stipulations with Relation to Chinese, a.k.a. the Chinese Exclusion Act, 1882: The Exclusion Act established a precedent for excluding or limiting immigration from Asian countries over the first decades of the 20th century. The first legislation to exclude immigrants on the basis of nationality, ethnicity, or race, it was directed at the Chinese. It prohibited Chinese laborers from entering the country for 10 years and reversed important sections of the Burlingame-Seward Treaty.

Foran Act Prohibiting Contract Labor, 1885: This act outlawed the payment of transportation costs for contract laborers prior to immigration. It was intended to limit Asian immigration beyond the Chinese Exclusion Act of 1882.

Hawaii Constitution, a.k.a the Bayonet Constitution, 1887: In addition to shifting economic and political power from the native monarchy to the U.S. government, it officially disenfranchised the Asian populations already present on the island and particularly the incoming Japanese émigrés. The constitution limited voting rights to native Hawaiians, Americans and Europeans, had a tax requirement, and required a reading test for men under the age of 47.

An Act to Prohibit the Coming of Chinese Laborers to the United States, a.k.a. the Scott Act, 1888: Intended to prevent reentry of those Chinese laborers who had temporarily returned to their homeland, the Scott Act was the next step toward ending all Chinese immigration. It rendered null and void the certificates secured by the laborers to ensure their lawful return.

An Act to Prohibit the Coming of Chinese Persons into the United States, a.k.a. the Geary Act, 1892: The act extended all appropriate legislation, including the Exclusion Act of 1882, for another 10 years, and required all Chinese to acquire certificates of eligibility within one year.

Treaty of Peace between the United States and Spain, a.k.a. the Treaty of Paris, 1898: The treaty gave the United States possession of Cuba, Puerto Rico, Guam, the Mariana Islands, and the Philippines in exchange for $20 million. This put the Filipinos under United States rule, after fighting side-by-side to remove Spanish control.

The Annexation of Hawaii, 1898: Despite not having the necessary two-thirds majority in the Senate to approve annexation, the Hawaiian territory was annexed all the same because of its strategic location and vulnerability to imperialists' powers. In the legislation, reference is made to the growing competition with Japan that would later affect Japanese Americans after the turn of the century.

An Act to Provide a Government for the Territory of Hawaii, a.k.a. the Organic Act of 1900: The act formally made Hawaii a territory of the United States and all citizens subject to U.S. laws. It provided U.S.

citizenship for all recognized residents of Hawaii as of the annexation of 1898 and those born on the Islands after annexation.

Executive Order No. 589, a.k.a the Gentlemen's Agreement, 1907: Through a series of notes exchanged between the United States and Japanese governments, Japan agreed to stop issuing passports for laborers seeking to go to America. Parents, spouses, and children of Japanese already in the country were allowed to emigrate. The Executive Order was intended to quell anti-Japanese sentiment in California, while maintaining good relations with Japan. The order stopped short of passing legislation barring immigration, mollifying the Japanese government, a growing power in Asia and the Pacific.

The Immigration Act of 1917, a.k.a. the Barred Zone Act: Using circumlocution— avoiding direct reference to the excluded nations and nationalities—the act bars the immigration of peoples between specific longitudes and latitudes. The established "zone" included all of South Asia, parts of Russia and the Middle East, Afghanistan, and the Polynesian islands. Because it was a United States territory, the Philippines was exempt from the act.

The Emergency Quota Act, a.k.a. the Immigration Act of 1921: In response to increased immigration to the United States as a result of World War I, this act limited immigration to the U.S. to 3 percent of the number of persons from that country present as of the 1910 census. This act laid the groundwork for the National Origins Act of 1924.

An Act Relative to the Naturalization and Citizenship of Married Women, a.k.a. the Cable Act, 1922: The act decreed that United States female citizens would have their citizenship stripped if they married aliens ineligible for citizenship. The legislators and this legislation reflected the concerns about not only who entered the country, but how the aliens would alter the complexion of American society.

National Origins Act: An Act to Limit the Immigration of Aliens Into the United States, and for Other Purposes, a.k.a. the Immigration Act of 1924: This federal law set numeric quotas on foreign immigrants, defining the nation's immigration policy for much of the 20th century. The act discriminated against Asians and Pacific Islanders, excluding them as "aliens ineligible to citizenship."(Minimum quota of any nationality was 100.) In favoring northern and western Europeans, the act humiliated the expanding Japanese empire and may be viewed as an important link in a chain of events leading to the attack on Pearl Harbor.

The Tydings-McDuffie Act, a.k.a. the Philippines Independence Act, 1934: This legislation provided independence for the Philippines and moved them from "American nationals" into the category of "aliens ineligible for citizenship." The act ensured the continued privilege of United States business interests in the Philippines and limited Filipino immigration to the United States. The Tydings-McDuffie Act set an immigration quota of 50 Filipinos per year and was the end result of nearly 20 years of legislative maneuvering to end Filipino immigration while maintaining the United States' position in the Philippines.

Filipino Repatriation Act, 1935: As an attempt to encourage the emigration of the 45,000 remaining Filipinos throughout the United States, the act offered free transportation to any Filipino, except those in Hawaii, willing to return to Manila. Fewer than 2,200 accepted the offer.

Executive Order Authorizing the Secretary of War to Prescribe Military Areas, No. 9066, 1942: In response to the United States entrance into World War II, President Roosevelt authorized the Secretary of War to put areas under military authority. The effect of the order was that people of Japanese descent were removed from the coastal areas of the western United States. Executive Order 9066 is connected to several other laws that provided legal cover to forcibly relocate Japanese Americans to centers through the country.

Public Law 77-503, 1942: Enacted to support Executive Order 9066, the law made the violation of military orders a federal offense punishable with a $5,000 fine and one-year imprisonment.

An Act to Repeal the Chinese Exclusion Acts, to Establish Quotas, and Other Purposes, a.k.a. the Magnuson Act, 1943: President Roosevelt repealed the original 1882 Exclusion Act and all subsequent acts preventing the immigration of Chinese to the United States and naturalization of Chinese residents. This act was passed during World War II, marking a change in federal policy regarding Chinese in particular and Asians in general.

Public Law 79-271, a.k.a. the War Brides Act, 1945: This legislation provided for non quota admission of foreign women who married American servicemen overseas during and after World War II. This law affected Chinese American communities, where servicemen married Chinese women after World War II and during the Korean War.

Philippines Veterans Rescission Act, 1946: Over 400,000 Filipino veterans served in the U.S. Armed Forces during World War II. Congress passed an act that singled out Filipinos to be denied a variety of benefits received by other foreign troops who served. It is estimated that the monies due to Filipino servicemen for back pay under Missing Persons Act, mustering-out pay, and disability support may be in excess of $1 billion today.[1]

Filipino and Indian Immigration and Naturalization Act, a.k.a. the Luce-Cellar Act, 1946: The Filipino and Indian Immigration and Naturalization Act extended American citizenship to Filipino and Asian Indian residents in the United States who arrived prior to March 24, 1943. The immigration quota for each was increased to 100 people a year.

McCarran-Walter Immigration and Nationality Act, 1952: The act eliminated all restriction on naturalization of Japanese immigrants and equalized policies dealing with gender. It eliminated the "barred zone," but created the "Asia-Pacific Triangle," which kept quotas at 2,000 people total for the nineteen countries within the triangle.

An Act to Amend the Immigration and Nationality Act, and for Other Purposes, a.k.a. the Immigration and Nationality Act, 1965: The most far-reaching and important revision of American immigration policy since the Immigration Act of 1924, the act removed the discriminatory elements of the previous acts directed at people of color. Immigration was increased to a total of 170,000 per year, with 20,000 immigrants from each of the nations in the eastern hemisphere previously excluded. The act provided immigration and naturalization to relatives of United States citizens without quotas or limitations and was responsible for the rapid increase in the Asian American population in the United States since 1970.

Indochina Migration and Refugee Assistance Act, 1975: In response to the United States' retreat from Vietnam and the need to assist those in Vietnam, Cambodia, and Laos who supported the nation's effort, the Indochina Migration and Refugee Assistance Act sought to provide for resettlement of the refugees in receiving or staging centers throughout the United States. In the 10 years following the act, 750,000 refugees entered the country.

Public Law 100-204, sections 904, 905, and 906, a.k.a. Southeast Asian Refugee Acts, 1987: These acts expanded upon the Indochina Refugee Act of 1975 by addressing Vietnamese, Laotian, and Cambodian refugees in the asylum camps throughout Thailand and other Southeast Asian countries and the relocation of the refugees to the United States. The acts acknowledged the need to provide entry to children born to American fathers and Vietnamese mothers.

Public Law 1000-383, a.k.a. the Civil Liberties Act, 1988: Twenty years of agitation on behalf of those Japanese Americans interned in World War II led to passage of the Civil Liberties Act. The act provided for an official apology from the Federal Government and a redress payment of $20,000 for each internee alive at the time of signing. Aleut Indians, who were also removed from their homelands for military purposes, received $12,000 for each survivor. Surviving Japanese Latin Americans interned in the United States later sued successfully for redress as well, and received $5,000 payments.

Executive Order Increasing Participation of Asian Americans and Pacific Islanders in Federal Programs, No. 13125, 1999: Representing the first executive order focusing on Asian Americans since Executive Order 9066, the directive established an interagency team and a Presidential Advisory Committee on Asian Americans and Pacific Islanders. It also solicited data on ways federal agencies might assist underserved Asian Pacific American communities.

Endnote
1. The figure of $1 billion comes from Franklin Odo, ed. *The Columbia Documentary History of the Asian American Experience* (New York: Columbia University Press, 2002), 320.

Bibliography
Chan, Sucheng. *Asian Americans: An Interpretative History*. Twayne's Immigrant History of America Series, New York: Twayne Publishing, 1991.

Odo, Franklin, ed. *The Columbia Documentary History of the Asian American Experience*. New York: Columbia University Press, 2002.

Thernstrom, Stephen, ed. *Harvard Encyclopedia of American Ethnic Groups*. Cambridge, MA: Belknap Press, 1980.

Index

Eskimo-Aleut migration, 21n1

Espina, Marina, 65

Espiritu, Yen Le, 24n33, 25n52, 25n53, 65

ethnicity, definitions, 21

Exclusion Act of 1882, 46, 52

Executive Order 589 (a.k.a. Gentlemen's Agreement, 1907), 9, 10, 22n22, 68

Executive Order 9066 (1942), 9, 32, 62, 69

Executive Order 13125 (1999), 70

exhumation, 54n7, 60

F

Fafai Beach Site, 58

Faga Village Site, 57

faluw, 57

Farrell, Mary M., 66

Federal Writers' Projects (WPA), 54n4

Filipino and Indian Immigration and Naturalization Act (a.k.a. Luce-Cellar Act, 1946), 70

Filipino Repatriation Act (1935), 69

Filipino Social Club, 30

Filipino Varsity Four, 3

Filipinos
    agriculture and, 2, 3, 11, 60
    Bainbridge Island Filipino Community Hall, 60
    census, U.S. (2000), 7, 11
    fishing industry, 30-31, 57
    immigration patterns, 11
    labor unions, 23
    sailors, 2, 21n11, 57
    soldiers, 3
    students (pensionados), 3

firebending, 49

fishing industry, 8, 30–31, 48–49, 55n12, 57, 62

Flores, Pedro, 4

Foran Act Prohibiting Contract Labor (1885), 67

Fort Sam Houston (Texas), 63

Fort Sill (Oklahoma), 63

Fort Snelling (Minnesota), 63

Fourteenth Amendment, U.S. Constitution, 34, 67

Fourth Army Intelligence School, 33

Friendship Archway, 13

Fujita, Jun, 28–29, 40n2, 60

funerary practices, 54n7, 57, 60

G

Gadao's Cave, 58

Gakuen Hall, 61

gardens
    Chinese, 45-46, 54n6, 59
    Japanese, 59, 63, 64

Guam, 5

Geary Act (1892), 68

Gentlemen's Agreement of 1907, 9, 10, 22n22, 68

gold rush, 8, 46, 57, 64

Golden Spike National Historic Site, 60

Gong Lum, et al v. Rice, et al, 34

Grace Quan, 49, 55n1

Graves, Donna, 18, 25n44, 40n12, 65

Guam, 9, 11, 23, 58

"Guardian of the West Gate", 52

gum saan ("Gold Mountain"), 8

H

haiku, 28, 40n1

Hanalei National Wildlife Reserve, 46–47

Hanalei Pier, 38, 64

Harada House, 61

Haraguchi Rice Mill, 46–47, 55n9, 58

Hawaii/Hawaiians,
    agriculture, 2, 8-11, 13, 38, 41n24, 46-47, 58, 64
    census, U.S. (2000), 6, 7
    fishing, 62
    historic sites, 6, 13, 27, 29-30, 38, 46-47, 58-59, 62-63, 64
    laws and legislation, 67, 68, 69
    religious sites, 13-14, 29-30, 58-59, 63
    secret societies – 6, 58
    settlement in, 6, 12, 22n13, 22n14, 23n29

Hawaii Constitution (a.k.a. Bayonet Constitution, 1887), 67

Hawaii Shingon Mission, 58

Hegemony, 22n22, 23n28

heiaus, 63

highway projects, 9, 22n19, 24n38

Hinduism, 12, 64

Sikh faith, 10

Singapore, 5

Solomon Islands, 23n23

South Dakota, 9

Southeast Asia Refugee Acts (1987), 70

Southeast Asian Water Festival, 14, 44, 54n3

Stedman-Thomas Historic District, 27, 30–31, 40n7, 40n8, 57

sugar industry, 8, 9–10, 13, 41n24

syncretism, 20

T

Tacoma Japanese Language School, 61

Taiwan, 5, 23n29

Takahashi Farm, 17, 24n38

Takaki, Ronald, 66

tanka (poetry), 28, 40n1

Taoist architecture, 64

Tchen, John Kuo Wei, 66

tea houses, 63, 64

Teaching with Historic Places, 50–51

Texas, 3, 7, 63

Thailand, 5

Thais, 7

theaters, 59, 61

theme studies, 32–35

Thernstrom, Stephen, 71

tong houses, 6, 58

torii, 30

Toyo Theatre, 59

Traditional Cultural Properties (TCPs), 24

transcontinental railroad, 2, 8, 60, 63

Treaty of Peace between the United States and Spain (a.k.a. Treaty of Paris,1898), 68

Tydings-McDuffie Act (a.k.a Philippines Independence Act, 1934), 69

U

Umatac Outdoor Library, 58

Upton, Dell, 66

U.S. Army 100th Battalion, 51

U.S. Army 442nd Regimental Combat Team, 3, 51

U.S. Constitution, Fourteenth Amendment, 34, 67

U.S. Fish and Wildlife Service, 46–47

U.S. Fourth Army Command, 32-33

U.S. Immigration Station (Angel Island), 51–53

U.S. Supreme Court Building, 62

Utah, 60

V

Vedanta Society, 12, 64

Vietnam, 5

Vietnamese, 3, 7, 44, 54n1, 70

Virginia, 7

Voyagers National Park, 28

W

Wailua Complex of Heiaus, 63

Wakamiya Inari Shrine, 27, 29-30, 59

Walnut Grove Chinese American Historic District, 62

Walnut Grove Japanese American Historic District, 62

War Brides Act of 1945, 22, 70

"War Relocation Camps" lesson plans, 50-51

Warren Mining District, 17, 24n38, 45–46, 54–55, 59-60

Washington, 6, 9-10, 12, 17, 57, 60–61, 64

water festival, 14, 44, 54n3,

Wegars, Priscilla, 19, 25n51, 66

Weiss, Alexander, 52

Western Defense Command (WDC), 32, 62

Wing Luke Asian Museum, 46

Wo Hing Society Building, 58

Women's Army Corps, 51

"Wonder of the Pacific", 31

Works Progress Administration (WPA), 54n4

World War II, 3, 9, 10, 15, 29, 40, 50-52, 62

worship, buildings and sites, 12-14, 27, 29-30, 35-36, 57-60, 63-64

WPA Federal Writers' Projects, 54n4

Wyoming, 50–51

Y

Yasui v. United States (1943), 62

Yip, Christopher, 17, 25n43

yo-yo, 4

yoga, 4

Illustrations

The Grace Quan sails San Francisco Bay, 49

Japanese Americans at Manzanar, attending classes in 1943, 50

I Rei To, or the soul-consoling tower, 50

The Rohwer Veterans Memorial in Arkansas, 51

Angel Island Immigration Station, 52

Angel Island Immigration Station – Chinese carved poems that became part of the historic record of the immigration station, 53